D0791909

American Government
....Like it is

Jack Anderson
Carl Kalvelage

American Government
....Like it is

Jack Anderson
Carl Kalvelage

GENERAL LEARNING PRESS

Printed in the United States of America.

Library of Congress Card Number: 73-185109

ISBN 0-382-18034-8

2013020

*If there be a country in the
world where the doctrine of
the sovereignty of the people ...
can be studied in its appli-
cation to the affairs of
society — and where its
dangers and advantages may
be judged — that country is
assuredly America.*
— *Alexis de Tocqueville,
1831*

Contents

INTRODUCTION

This work is a supplement, a booster shot for the American Government text your instructor has selected. That text will tell you in detail how the government is supposed to operate; we will try to "tell it like it is." The two versions are not often in perfect alignment—in fact, in some areas they don't even touch.

The text, for instance, will tell you that a Congressman's salary is $42,500. This book will take it from there and explain that certain Congressmen support a lifestyle so lush that $42,500 would barely cover their board and lodging. The Congressmen, therefore, m   nding money beyond their basic salary. We'll take you an   and pinpoint the sources of their extra money, and explain ho.   sources can constitute a conflict of interest wherein the Congressmen end up representing their pocketbooks rather than their constituents.

The formal text, after all, is a blueprint of American government. It shows the structure and superstructure, the stress points and joists, the dimensions to scale. All very accurate, but all falling short of the mark. Blueprints are bloodless, whereas Presidents are men; senators are men; judges are men. American government is a government of flesh and blood, and until a student can see for himself how different men bend the blueprint to their ends, the study of government will be at best abstract, at worst, irrelevant.

This supplement is written to help you find some relevancy—to hang the flesh on the skeleton of theory. Men being what they are, it is to be expected that along with relevancy will come some degree of disenchantment and bitterness. This is a sign of health, not sickness—sign of scales falling from the eyes. It is rather like growing up and suddenly realizing that the parents whom we loved were not at all infallible; that they were, instead, often petty and pretentious and sometimes selfish and thoughtless. In other words, that they were human. But the initial shock wore off and we loved them just as much. More perhaps, since now we understand them better.

So it is with the American system of government—a system as petty as an aging dowager, pretentious as a used car salesman—but it's a very human system and we've grown to love it.

In these pages we try to throw some light on the hidden side of government, the side most people don't often get to see. Scholars will look in vain for the sources. We have named only those bold enough to speak on the record. Most of the information came to us confidentially, often from people who have an intense aversion to publicity. This isn't to say that the informants are furtive types who meet in back alleys and whisper cryptic messages out of the corner of their mouths. The best material has come from Presidents, Cabinet officers, members of Congress, generals and admirals. The higher their rank, the less anxious they are, usually, to be quoted. Some of the information is drawn from the files of the syndicated newspaper column "Washington Merry-Go-Round"; some has been developed from new investigations made especially for this book. All of it can be documented.

Readers may attempt to find partisan political significance in this supplement, but if there is an imbalance that favors one party over the other, it is unintentional. It is simply a sad fact that men in both parties work hard to preserve the weaknesses in the governmental system, weaknesses that make abuses possible. This book points out many of those weaknesses; the class text describes the strengths. The student, to see American government like it is, must know about both.

CONGRESS

Long jaded by exposure to pretenders to greatness, the unenfranchised residents of the District of Columbia still find the view of the Capitol dome inspiring in the morning light. The dome is the symbol of man's most intensive effort to subject the function of governing to the will of the governed—a cathedral to the memory of the nation's founders, a breast to nourish the hopes of Americans who will follow. But Washington's neoclassic temples of government shelter petty thieves and bold brigands—the political Pharisees of modern America.

It would be as naive to suppose that the members of the United States Senate and House of Representatives are unaware of the dark stains on their institutions as it would be to pretend that all of them entered politics out of a genuine fervor for public service. Politics is as honorable a career as any other. Yet the honorable men in Congress demean themselves by ignoring the corruption that flourishes in their midst. Many members who might be tempted to speak out against the abuses around them find they cannot. They have been compromised by the small favors they have done, or intimidated by the wielders of power, or bought off by the necessity of seeking funds for re-election, or hushed by a code of comradeship that ignores morality. Their silence is complicity in the deeds of the corrupt.

Congressmen, no matter how lofty their motives, have been flattered into believing that they are different from the rest of us, as if the process of election has somehow lifted them above other Americans and made them more knowing, more worthy and less subject to reproach than the people who elect them. Congressmen, too, can easily become insulated from the world around them. Their office staffs act as buffers between them and disagreeable news; the aides who have survived are those who have learned not to make waves. Wherever Congressmen go, they are treated with adulation. Many ordinary men among them are lulled into believing they receive this treatment because they deserve it, and even those who resist the narcotic of flattery are not entirely immune to the heady atmosphere on Capitol Hill.

There are no guides to the real workings of Congress. Least instructive of all, perhaps, is the literature offered to tourists. The seating charts available to visitors in the galleries of the Senate and House chambers are not footnoted to explain to the casual observer the hidden interests, the friendships, the ambitions, the power relationships, the economic dependencies, the political pressures, or the personal prejudices that motivate the men who suddenly appear on the floor, conduct their business, and just as suddenly disappear.

WHAT YOU DO FOR YOUR CONGRESSMAN

A casual tour of the congressional compound can be somewhat more enlightening about the atmosphere in which Congress lives than a guided tour. The unescorted visitor will encounter the spoils system—a system contrived, that is, to spoil the Congressmen. Elevators in the Senate wing, marked SENATORS ONLY, quickly impress the anointed with their own importance. More regal, perhaps, is the treatment of Senators in their office building elevators. They can summon immediate service by pushing the bell three times. Other passengers are ignored by the college students who man the lifts; a Senator's command is the operator's only priority. Indeed, the ancillary benefits of election to Congress are overwhelming. Taken individually, many of these prizes can be excused as the trappings of rank. As a whole, they form a pattern of living that can be likened to the excesses of the Roman emperors, whose palaces gave birth to the architectural form of Capitol Hill. Behind these walls Congress has created a citadel of privilege.

The Senate alone has spawned a dozen restaurants to feed its members and its workers on meals subsidized for $497,000 by the taxpayers in the latest budget year. It also provides a beauty salon and a number of barbershops for employees where the price is about half what a haircut costs elsewhere in Washington. When the fee was raised from $1.25 to $2, there were cries of anguish from the pampered patrons. Only the Senators did not complain; they have their own private barbershop where the haircuts are free.

The Senate stationery shop is a drab basement room that has unusual appeal for Senators and their staffs. The store has nothing but bargains, since all items are sold at their wholesale cost. There is no markup for overhead or salaries. Besides office supplies, the store provides items like cut-rate Christmas cards and engraved wedding invitations for its patrons. This basement bargain counter at one time purveyed auto tires and whiskey to its select clientele, but the rules were finally stiffened when the stock list became an embarrassment to the Senate.

Other rooms are dedicated to the further comfort and convenience of Senators. The Senate has its own shops for carpentry, electrical work, and, to insure that Senatorial bottoms are properly cushioned, upholstery work. There are also steam baths to help Senators recover from the after-hours duties of their office, and two swimming pools where they can cavort in the nude to soothe tired muscles.

On the House side of Capitol Hill, Representatives enjoy similar privileges in their own cloistered surroundings, often with embellishments designed to compensate for the inferiority complex felt by House members who have neither the prestige nor the power of the Senate. The behemoth Rayburn House Office Building is a monument to self-indulgence. The design and appointments reflect both a lack of taste and a lack of propriety, and its $122 million cost—the highest price tag in history for an office building—demonstrates the members' low regard for the public. The building, completed in 1965, is named for the late Speaker Sam Rayburn, and he is blamed for most of its extravagances. Representatives who have offices in the monstrosity will admit privately, however, that they enjoy its comforts.

No one would deny Congressmen sufficient office space to house their staffs. Before the Rayburn Building was completed, some House offices were crowded to the bursting point. Representative Dante Fascell (D-Fla.) conscientious about his responsibility to a million citizens of the Miami area, had to move desks for secretaries inside his own private office and store his files in the bathroom. For a while, he had a woman working in the narrow corridor that led to the bathroom, but she was pregnant, and gave up her job when she could no longer squeeze into her chair space.

Such a problem, however, did not justify a vulgar, $122 million building with a $9.3 million parking lot for 1,220 cars, a 20-by-60-foot indoor swimming pool, a gymnasium, offices equipped with private kitchens, plus a 700-seat cafeteria and five dining rooms. There have been numerous charges of political payoffs in the construction of the building, but little evidence has been offered other than the fact that Matt McCloskey, a former treasurer of the Democratic National Committee, was the builder. A greater crime than the possible financial chicanery, however, is the damage the building has done to the reputation of

Congress, just by its existence. Its false grandeur fails to inspire confidence in the ability of Congress to manage the affairs of the nation, and serves to perpetuate the caricature of Congressmen as luxury-loving, free-spending wastrels who are for sale to the highest bidders. Such an image is unquestionably unfair to many hardworking men who are true to their convictions and honest in their dealings. For many, service in Congress is both a personal sacrifice and a proud honor. For others, however, the caricature fits.

By itself, the $42,500 annual salary paid to members of Congress is modest enough. Those who have been required to live on their salaries believe it is just about right. "I don't think that a Congressman should get too far from the people in what he earns," explained Paul Douglas, who, until his defeat by Charles Percy, was the Democratic Senator from Illinois. But less scrupulous legislators have discovered a dozen ways to skin the taxpayers. The unpublicized but officially countenanced benefits of membership in Congress are worth noting.

Pensions. Since even a Southern district on occasion has been known to throw out its Representative, Congress has provided a pension plan for those who fail to get re-elected. It has all manner of clauses rarely found in a private industry contract. By contributing 8 per cent of his annual emolument, the 30-year man can qualify for as much as $31,875 a year. Pensions are also paid on top of any Social Security or private retirement plans. To become eligible, the politician pensioner need serve only five years in Congress.

Tax Break. A Congressman who maintains two houses—one in Washington, another in his home state—pays no federal income tax on up to $3,000 of his $42,500 income.

Stationery Allowance. Each Representative is allowed $3,500 during a session for the purchase of office supplies, including stationery. The allowance is credited to his account in the stationery rooms and may be withdrawn in cash or left to pay for office purchases. This is an allowance so curiously unrestricted that a Congressman may pocket the entire amount if he wishes. Senators are allowed $3,600, but since a 1969 amendment to the Public Law, the funds are simply available until expended.

Telephone and Telegraph Allowance. A Senator is now eligible for 3,000 free long-distance calls per year, plus $2,200 worth of calls originating and terminating outside of Washington, plus a telegram allowance based on the size of the state and its proximity to Washington.

For Senators from large states (over 10 million population), an additional 1,500 no-charge calls per year are permitted. Somewhat differently, both telephone calls and telegrams are lumped together in a House member's allowance under the quaintly arcane "unit" system. For each session of Congress, he receives 80,000 units. For every minute of long-distance chatter, he is charged with four units. Californians obviously get more for their "units" than do Marylanders, but it's the rare lawmaker who bleeds his account dry. Even so, for the particularly garrulous member who might find himself running short of units, there is yet another provision. This is the $150 backstop allowance, or what Oklahoma's former Senator Mike Monroney has called a "sort of slop-over deal." Senior members may also arrange to charge their excess phone calls to the committees on which they serve. An even greater largess recently granted Congressmen is the FTS or Federal Telephone System, under which a Senator may call any state lying between his and Washington as many times as he pleases free of charge. This service is restricted for Representatives to between 5 P.M. and 9 A.M. Again, Californians gain most from this setup.

District Allowance. The legislator's political radar is located in his district office, for which there is also an allowance. Each member is entitled to office space at not more than two places within his constituency. The Sergeant at Arms will arrange for comfortable quarters in some handy federal building. But if this is not available, a member may look elsewhere for space. Rep. Alvin O'Konski (R-Wis.) found rental space in his own radio station, WLIN in Merrill, Wis.; the late Rep. William Dawson (D-Ill.) drew $100 a month to pay office rent in the Second Ward Democratic headquarters on Chicago's South Side. Rep. Charles Diggs, Jr. (D-Mich.) paid $75 a month rental to Diggs Enterprises, Inc., of Detroit. And the list can go on. In each case, the rent was paid by the government.

Travel Allowance. Congress has increased the transportation allowance of a Senator from six to twelve round trips home each year; of a Representative from four to twelve round trips. Twenty cents a mile is also paid for one more round trip, calculated separately. Even so, this is a woefully small allowance. "Four trips a year may have been all right during the railroad age," grumbled one Senator, "but this is a jet era, and I have to fly home thirty times a year." Because the allotment is scant, the mischief is often considerable. Once the travel kitty has dried up, some Congressmen will contrive to go home by any means except one that is paid for out of their own pockets. Every Friday, a fleet of corporation-owned planes is available to whisk Congressmen home for the weekend—a handy service that often pays high legislative dividends to the owners of those planes.

House Folding Room.   The modern lawmaker uses tons of paper. What he decides to put on it, or how much he sends as frankable mail, is a secret the House Folding Room will never reveal. Eli Bjellos, generalissimo in charge of this subterranean operation, says there is no limit to the amount of "bulk printed matter" a Congressman may send out. As long as it is frankable, he will fold, insert or wrap it for immediate mailing.

Senate Service Department.   It is a rule of thumb that anything a Representative must buy for a pittance is available free to a Senator. To implement this dictum, Congress has created the Senate Service Department. Its origins are obscure, its services secret. Behind unmarked doors in the Old Senate Office Building, this department is supposed to operate on a nonprofit basis. Insiders claim that the salaries of at least 60 employees—including truck drivers, messengers and offset press operators—are camouflaged in the over-all budget of the Senate Sergeant at Arms.

Map Service.   Free maps of all sizes and shapes, either for personal use or for mailing to constituents are available to members.

Binding Service.   For those afflicted by pride of authorship, Congress provides that "Members may have any public document, which has been published during their term of office, bound in a fine permanent binding by the Government Printing Office."

Recording Studios.   Both the Senate and House provide radio and television studios, the latter equipped with sets that rival anything on the Warner Brothers lot. The most often used set is the congressional office, designed in boardroom motif, with a stunning view of the Capitol dome beneath a bank of cumulus clouds. Both studios charge less than $20 to make a five-minute television film, which is about $380 less than a commercial outfit would charge. (The late Senator Everett Dirksen (R-Ill.) gained an advantage over other recording stars by cutting his profitable, patriotic recording of "Gallant Men" in the tax-subsidized Senate studios.)

Franking Privilege.   Despite a generous stamp allowance, Congressmen are also granted the franking privilege, which permits them merely to sign their first-class mail. A House member gets 40,000 speech-sized envelopes, all duly franked, for mailing out copies of his speeches; a Senator is allotted 60,000. Though speech-sized envelopes are rationed, letter-sized ones have no limitation. Under the law, franked material must be "official correspondence"; however, the Post Office accepts a broad definition.

Printing Shops. Deep in the ink-splattered rooms of the Old House Office Building are two printing shops run by David Ramage, who is listed on the House rolls as "majority clerk," and Thomas Lankford, "minority clerk." Their titles allow them to be carried on the payroll of the House Sergeant at Arms. Needless to say, they pass their bargains on to the Congressmen. Two photographers are also provided by the taxpayers to record such historic events as the Millville High School's senior class calling on their Congressman.

Library of Congress. In addition to all the books a Congressman can borrow, the Library of Congress also provides a Legislative Reference Service whose 360 harried researchers will check out anything from the number of koala bears in Australia to the pesticides best suited for the truck gardens of Matsuyama. Upon request, the researchers will spend up to 50 hours on a single project. LRS handles upwards of 180,000 Congressional inquiries a year. And while on the subject, here is a little story about the Library of Congress and congressional privilege that bears retelling.

Deep in the recesses of the Library of Congress, a team of skilled professionals restores and preserves historic documents for the library's famous collection. In the past few years, they have worked on the papers of such men as Thomas Jefferson and Woodrow Wilson. But for a considerable part of 1970 they were obliged to give valuable attention to more dubious documents of a different kind. Senator Strom Thurmond, the indomitable old man from South Carolina who has become a power with the Nixon Administration, decided he wanted some of his personal papers preserved for posterity. So he turned over to the Library such historical gems as a certificate of Thurmond's membership in the 82nd Airborne Division Association and a copy of his routine authorization to practice law before the Fourth Judicial Circuit.

Despite the uncertain national value of the Thurmond papers, the library was not about to turn Thurmond down. For one thing, he served on the joint House-Senate Committee on the library's administration. Explained Frazier Poole, head of the library's preservation department, "We get asked once in a while to oblige a Congressman, and if it won't interfere with our work, we do it." A library staffer told newsmen that he could remember only one other senatorial request in recent years. Then, he said, only a single document was involved. So the library put 23 of the Thurmond documents through its costly special process. For some reason, it declined to process certificates proclaiming "Strom Thurmond Day" in Shreveport and Bossier City, Louisiana. It may be worth mentioning that when newsmen called Thurmond's office regarding his library caper, the Senator immediately sent a check to the library to cover the cost of the work.

Parking.   For 100 Senators, there is free underground parking for about 400 cars. The 435 House members have 1,600 parking spaces underground. Congressional employees use free outdoor lots and reserved spaces on the streets. But the prerogative extends far beyond this. Members of Congress are exempt from parking restrictions when on official business. Over the years, the area of immunity has broadened to include their families, staffs and often visiting constituents as well. Former Senator Wayne Morse, the vigilant Oregonian, once fumed that 33,739 tickets were fixed in a single year. When the District of Columbia commissioners threatened to change the rules to make the streets passable during the rush hours, however, they were hauled before the House District of Columbia Committee and quickly humbled. The Washington National Airport reserves a section of parking area for Congressmen. This is a free service, too.

Health Care.   A Congressman growing green about the gills can call upon one of the three doctors in the Capitol for free medical advice. Most medicines, too, are absolutely free. If he needs hospitalization, he can check in at any military hospital and pay only for his board and room. The chief of the congressional medical staff is Dr. Rufus Pearson, who draws a $1,500 monthly expense allowance in addition to his Navy salary and commutes in a seven-passenger, air-conditioned government limousine, replete with chauffeur. Pearson's office handles 47,500 patient visits in an average year. He also supervises a pharmacy and a physical therapy room on Capitol Hill as well as a first-aid station staffed by a nurse in each congressional office building. A resuscitator is kept near each chamber, first-aid equipment and stretchers are available in the Democratic and Republican cloakrooms, and an ambulance is gassed and ready in the Senate garage for any emergency.

Miscellaneous.   Congressmen are supplied with all the free flowers and plants they can use, a gift of the National Botanical Gardens. Senators also are in line for an unlimited supply of carbonated water, the demand for which is immense, since one of the higher status drinks around the capital city is scotch or bourbon or whiskey and water.

Finally, one of the more prestigeous and negotiable privileges a Congressman boasts is his right to appoint five students to each of the three major military academies. Each of the 15 students attending these schools for four years receives an education with a dollar equivalent of $60,000.

This is what the taxpayer does for his Congressman; now it might be interesting to know what the Congressman can do for the taxpayer.

WHAT THE CONGRESSMAN CAN DO FOR YOU

For an eight-cent postage stamp, any citizen can buy the services of a $42,500-a-year combination legislator, messenger, expediter, trouble shooter, travel guide and information bureau. These are the sorts of chores routine to 435 Representatives and 100 Senators who represent the home folks in Congress. Their constituents' requests range from a list of "everything that hasn't been invented yet" to information on "how to build a pigpen."

A typical Congressman averages about 100 letters every working day while Congress is in session. (When it's out, he gets them at home.) He welcomes them. He may rebel at playing errand boy (he prefers to play statesman), but the mail gives him an insight into the voters' thinking and points up problems minor legislation might remedy. Even the errands are worth their weight in votes.

If one has a favor to ask, chances are he'll get the better service from his Representative because a Rep's constituency is smaller than a Senator's. But even he can't do the impossible; he hasn't got all the keys and answers. One legislator has estimated he accomplishes about one-half of one per cent of what people expect. He can't, for instance, land a government contract for you, or juggle the Army around to suit you, or send you all the Supreme Court decisions back to 1860. But there are hundreds of services he can provide. Here are a few:

He can expedite claims or applications before the federal government.

He can send free government pamphlets on a variety of subjects. (Most popular: *Infant Care,* published by the Children's Bureau.)

He can ask the National Archives to help trace your family tree.

He can act as your counsel before federal boards (in a veteran's appeal case, for example).

He can introduce private legislation in hardship cases.

He may find you a patronage job as a guard, elevator operator or handyman on Capitol Hill.

He might make your son a congressional page or appoint him to West Point or Annapolis, if he qualifies.

If you have business in Washington, he can introduce you to the right official.

If you come to sightsee, he can supply you with passes to watch Congress in action, inspect the White House or take a conducted tour of the National Art Gallery.

He can hand out a few tickets to the Army-Navy football game, but he has to pay for these himself.

He can answer almost any question by asking the right government agency.

If you have a relative in a distant federal jail, he may get him transferred to a prison nearer your home. Or he can sometimes put in a good word with the federal board of parole.

He can even find an overcoat lost in the labyrinth of the U.S. Navy. Take Charles Bennett (D-Fla.) who heard that a hitchhiking constituent had left his overcoat in a sailor's car that was headed for Pensacola. "Mr. Congressman," the coatless constituent wrote, "the Navy has given me the brushoff. They say they can't find my coat. I don't think they even tried. Can you possibly help me?" Congressman Bennett had only to express "interest" to the Navy and within five days the coat was on its way to its owner.

A Congressman is a sort of congressional whiz kid, ready to answer the wildest questions. Generally, if your query has a serious answer, he'll try to find it. There was one, however, that stumped former Rep. John Vorys (R-Ohio): "How can you tell a horse's age by the bones in his tail?" Probably Vorys' most sweeping request came from a college coed who wrote blandly, "I'm studying government. Please send me everything that goes out of your office."

A Congressman's average day's mail runs something like this:

50 personal problems from constituents.
25 letters on legislation ("Do you favor the draft law?").
15 requests for pamphlets, bulletins and maps.
10 miscellaneous missives, such as form letters, anonymous gripes, etc. (Form letters receive form replies; anonymity usually remains unknown, unnoticed.)

The Congressman's staff spends about 90 per cent of its time answering these letters.

The Congressman, himself, must spend more of his time at the job he was elected to do — legislating. He must attend endless hearings, read stacks of legislative material, follow the floor debates. "A Congressman has another constituency," said the late House Speaker Sam Rayburn, "his colleagues in Congress. If he cooperates with them, he's in a better position to serve his constituency back home."

Most Congressmen want to perform such chores for their constituents. The problem is how to divide their time between legislation and running errands. Rep. F. Edward Hebert (D-La.) has this philosophy, developed over his long tenure in office:

"I was elected to legislate, but I'm lucky to spend 10 per cent of my time at it. I spend the other 90 per cent giving services to my constituents. The Congressman is a doorman to the big government bureaucracies in

Washington. He opens the door to let in the constituent who has a perfect right to get in by himself but is often kept out by the bureaucrats. The big tycoon pays up to $100,000 a year to have someone here looking after his interests. The little guy pays only his taxes. Yet the high-salaried lobbyist can't accomplish for the tycoon what one lowly Congressman can do for his petitioners."

Now, if Mr. Hebert — who has been on Capitol Hill for over 25 years — feels obliged to employ the phrase "lowly Congressman," how must the newcomer to the Senate or House of Representatives feel? How much weight can he hope to swing; how much help can he hope to be to his constituents?

ADVICE TO FRESHMEN

In the backrooms on Capitol Hill, the new Members who are sworn in every other January, must go through the initiation process. They are taken aside by their elders for a few words of quiet advice. The way to get ahead, they're told, is to hang back. Follow your leaders. Wait for their signals. The first freshman to poke his head above the crowd, they're cautioned, will receive only lumps. The golden orator, even while voicing a great truth, can hurt his cause. For the most effective speeches are delivered, not on the Senate floor or before the television cameras, but in the privacy of the cloakrooms.

The droning, out-of-context oratory in the congressional chambers has little to do with the legislative process. The great decisions are made in the policy huddles and shaped in the hard slog of the committee rooms. Even more important, the decisions are determined by the hidden interests, the friendships, the ambitions, the power relationships, the economic dependencies, the political pressures, the personal prejudices and the campaign obligations of the men who inhabit Capitol Hill.

For newcomers who seek admittance to the inner circle, who wish to become effective in the backrooms, here's the advice their leaders offer:

1. A Congressman who wants to leave his mark must be willing to work. He must tend to his committee chores and accept his share of legislative drudgery. In hearings, he should dig for facts, stick to the issues and not raise irrelevancies. "An effective Congressman," a committee chairman is fond of repeating, "is a working Congressman."

2. He must be flexible. While he should have convictions, he should be able, on occasion, to yield gracefully and to have a clear eye for the political realities. As one Democratic leader has put it to the newly elected, "You shouldn't be too violently addicted to principle."

3. He should avoid becoming a pop-off. The gadfly who seeks the spotlight is resented and is, therefore, ineffective. As one leader expresses it, "The fellow who behaves like the son of a wild jackass and fills the air with his braying may get his name in the papers but not on legislation."

4. He should become a specialist. The legislative circus under the Big Dome has so many acts all going on at the same time that it's impossible to star in all of them. The Congressman who becomes an expert in one field swings the most weight and, ultimately, his prestige will carry over into other fields.

5. He must be trustworthy. The backstab, a familiar method of advancement in politics, is unpardonable in the hallowed halls of Congress. The man who double-crosses his colleagues or gains political advantage at their expense soon finds himself an outsider.

6. He must be willing to make deals. To win support for his own legislation, he must trade votes, grant political IOU's, share credit and, when the occasion demands, come to the aid of his party. In the words of a wise, old GOP veteran, "To be effective with your colleagues, you must be prepared to scratch their particular itches. If you do, they will scratch yours."

THE SENILITY SYSTEM

The new Members never become really effective until they become old Members. This partiality for old age is referred to in American government texts as the seniority system. We call it the senility system.

When John F. Kennedy spoke boldly at his inauguration of the torch of leadership being passed to a new generation, the Congressional hierarchy, grouped in an arc behind him according to seniority, applauded tolerantly. But his words had no effect upon them. Congress has continued to be a council of elders, dominated by tired old men whose only claim to power is their good fortune in seldom facing serious opposition at election time.

The congressional seniority system hands command of the committees of the Senate and House to these men, regardless of their ability, honesty or even their possible senility. The system has produced chairmen who are not representative of the country's geography, its desires, its politics or its people· men who are out of step with the times and, often, with both the national Administration and the majority of their own members.

Committee chairmen have the power — and they use it — to appoint subcommittees, to decide when and whether committee meetings will be held, to hire committee staffs, to set hearings, to choose the witnesses who will appear, to call up the bills for floor action, to have the first and last words in debate. And finally, the chairmen of these various committees are the ones who select the conference groups that resolve the differences between Senate and House versions of legislation.

What this means is that however the ballots are cast in future elections, the voters are likely to exercise only a limited influence on legislation, for the Congress will be dominated by old men who march in slow cadence behind the nation. The committee chairmen of both the Senate and House average more than 65 years of age, most of them come from small towns or rural areas, and most are Southerners. In the Senate, 10 of the 17 chairmen are from the South, the rest from the West, or Midwest, with but one from the East. Although 65 is often the mandatory retirement age in private industry, 10 of the Senate chairmen are past the age; 6 of these are past 70. The situation is much the same in the House, with 11 of the 21 chairmanships held by Representatives from Southern and Southwestern states; 12 past 65, 7 over 70 and only 2 under 60 years of age.

This is not to say that over the years the seniority system has not produced some committee chairmen who have been exceptional leaders. It has. It has also propelled some appalling misfits into positions of awesome responsibility. Two who come most quickly to mind in the latter category were foisted on the nation by the voters of rural South Carolina: the late L. Mendel Rivers and John L. McMillan.

There are older, more cantankerous Congressmen than these. For instance, 86-year-old Representative Barratt O'Hara (D-Ill.), though venerated by his colleagues, had a short fuse and more than once threatened to settle an argument with his fists. During an argument with another Congressman over the State Department budget, O'Hara challenged his colleague, "Let the gentleman come out and argue with our fists. I am willing to revert to fisticuffs even at my age on the issue that no dining room in the State Department is worth $250,000 of taxpayers' money to impress foreign diplomats."

Some men hold their ages, of course, better than others do. The late Senator Theodore F. Green (D-R.I.), for example, was 69 before he was elected to the Senate. When he retired at 93, he was still remarkably alert. He played a stiff set of tennis on his seventieth birthday, continued diving off the high board until his mid-80's and walked the 16 blocks to his Senate office until the day he retired. At his ninety-second birthday party he was still keen enough, when asked how it felt to be 92, to quip, "Not bad — considering the alternative." And in the end, he was alert enough to realize that old men ought to step aside when their age slows them down. Accordingly, he resigned the chairmanship of the Foreign Relations Committee when his eyes and ears began to fail him.

Sadly, most of the old men do not know when to quit. Most are more like the late beloved Speaker Joseph Martin (R-Mass.), who at 82 was so infirm that he needed canes and other aids simply to move around. He had a short attention span and muffled powers of sight and sound. Yet he still ran for re-election. In his case, the voters regretfully retired him.

The seniority system not only places the biggest burdens on the frailest shoulders; it also confers power on legislators who come from safe rural districts. Nine of the 17 Senate chairmen come from cities or towns with populations of less than 100,000; only five of the 21 House chairmen come from sizeable cities. The seniority system was responsible for placing James Eastland, a Mississippi segregationist, in charge of civil rights legislation. Indeed, seniority has given Southerners a domination over Congress, which thus operates not unlike a Union Army led by Confederate generals.

The following complete list of standing committee chairmen speaks for itself.

Standing Committee Chairmen of the Senate:
  Aeronautical and Space Sciences — Clinton P. Anderson, New Mexico
  Agriculture and Forestry — Herman E. Talmadge, Georgia
  Appropriations — Allen J. Ellender, Louisiana
  Armed Services — F. Edward Hebert, Louisiana
  Banking, Housing, and Urban Affairs — John J. Sparkman, Alabama
  Commerce — Warren G. Magnuson, Washington
  District of Columbia — Thomas F. Eagleton, Missouri
  Finance — Russell B. Long, Louisiana
  Foreign Relations — J. W. Fulbright, Arkansas
  Government Operations — John L. McClellan, Arkansas
  Interior and Insular Affairs — Henry M. Jackson, Washington
  Judiciary — James O. Eas.'and, Mississippi
  Labor and Public Welfare — Harrison A. Williams, Jr., New Jersey
  Post Office and Civil Service — Gale W. McGee, Wyoming
  Public Works — Jennings Randloph, West Virginia
  Rules and Administration — B. Everett Jordan, North Carolina
  Veterans' Affairs — Vance Hartke, Indiana
Standing Committee Chairmen of the House·
  Agriculture — W. R. Poage, Texas
  Appropriations — George H. Mahon, Texas
  Armed Services — F. Edward Hebert, Louisiana
  Banking and Currency — Wright Patman, Texas
  District of Columbia — John L. McMillan, South Carolina
  Education and Labor — Carl D. Perkins, Kentucky
  Foreign Affairs — Thomas E. Morgan, Pennsylvania
  Government Operations — Chet Holifield, California

House Administration — Wayne L. Hays, Ohio
Interior and Insular Affairs — Wayne N. Aspinall, Colorado
Internal Security — Richard H. Ichord, Missouri
Interstate and Foreign Commerce — Harley O. Staggers, West Virginia
Judiciary — Emanuel Celler, New York
Merchant Marine and Fisheries — Edward A. Garmatz, Maryland
Post Office and Civil Service — Thaddeus J. Dulski, New York
Public Works — John A. Blatnik, Minnesota
Rules — William M. Colmer, Mississippi
Science and Astronautics — George P. Miller, California
Standards of Official Conduct — Melvin Price, Illinois
Veterans' Affairs — Olin E. Teague, Texas
Ways and Means — Wilbur D. Mills, Arkansas

Most Congressmen do not continue to serve for the money. Most could retire on the pensions they have built up over the years. They stay on in the tenacious belief that they can last longer and serve better than the young upstarts who challenge them. They feel that the country needs them. It will take severe public pressure, indeed, to overcome the seniority system.

CONGRESSMEN GET ALL THE BREAKS

Young or old, the United States Congressman is a privileged person; he gets all the breaks and if he should miss one, by chance, he is not above legislating the break for himself.

In 1960, John F. Kennedy aroused the spirit of sacrifice in America when he spoke his inaugural words, "Ask not what your country can do for you, ask what you can do for your country." Within ten years the watchword in Washington changed. The public was still asked to sacrifice, to hold down wage demands, to wait for promised better times. But they were expected to ask not that their leaders make similar sacrifices.

George Romney, the Secretary of Housing and Urban Development, made a brave attempt to set an example by turning back 25 per cent of his salary. When he suggested that his fellow cabinet officers do the same, however, he didn't get a single volunteer. Instead, the cabinet members accepted a salary increase from $35,000 to $60,000.

President Nixon, whose own pay had been raised from $100,000 to $200,000, dispatched his chief lobbyist to Capitol Hill to seek an increase also in the presidential pension from $25,000 to $60,000. Lobbyist Bryce Harlow slipped around to see then Speaker John McCormack who obligingly pushed the increase through the House and then quickly through the Senate. The Nixon sales pitch on the action was that he really wanted the extra pension for poor old Harry Truman. But at 87, Truman won't be around long enough to collect much of it. The real beneficiary will be Richard Nixon.

In the same spirit of self service, House leaders also arranged a little going-away present for the retiring McCormack. They cooked up a resolution that would grant "Old Jawn" a two-year lease on his present Boston office, $1,200 a year for office expenses, $3,000 a year for stationery, free mailing privileges, $700 extra for airmail and special delivery stamps, a $27,000-a-year assistant and a $12,000 secretary. There was even some talk about tossing in the use of a chauffeured government limousine.

When the story leaked to newspapers, the Speaker got hold of his old friend, House Administration Chairman Sam Friedel (D-Md.), who was in charge of the special resolution, and suggested magnanimously that he could struggle along without the airmail and special delivery stamps. He also thought his staff could get by on less pay. And never mind the limousine; his assistant could drive him around.

As a Christmas bonus for themselves in 1970, House members voted to increase their stationery allowance from $3,000 to $3,500 apiece. The extra allotment has cost the taxpayer as much as $218,000 each session. And some of the Congressmen wonder why the young people, who were truly stirred by President Kennedy's appeal, have soured on his heirs. Well, here are some other reasons.

COAST GUARD TAXI SERVICE

"Semper paratus," the Coast Guard motto, means "always ready." Lately, it has meant "always ready" to fly government bigwigs around in pleasure planes. The Coast Guard's Grumman Gulfstream II, executive jetliner, and Gulfstream I, propjet, are gleaming white on the outside with plush interiors befitting Aristotle Onassis. The jetliner is used by Transportation Secretary John Volpe, the Coast Guard's boss, as his personal plane. When he is seized with the urge to see the Paris Air Show or visit the Spanish Riviera, he is whisked in his government limousine to the ramp of his Goast Guard jet, then is flown in style wherever he may yearn to go. Thus, he avoids the transportation problems he is supposed to solve for the millions of less-blessed Americans.

But one can have no idea how many Congressmen and cabinet members have received the same VIP service until he is shown the logs for the two Coast Guard planes. The secret passenger roster reads like Who's Who in Washington. Some of the flights appear to be vaguely official but economically questionable. It costs more than $650 an hour to keep the jet in the air; more than$300 an hour to fly the propjet.

One frequent passenger is Rep. Frank Bow (R-Ohio), a power on the House Appropriations Committee, who is given to loud complaints about government spending. But not a whimper has been heard from him about the high cost of the Coast Guard pleasure flights. The logs show that the Coast Guard has flown Bow to or from Florida on several occasions, not to mention a trip home to Ohio, all at the taxpayers' expense. He told newsmen his trips have always been on official business, although he serves on no subcommittees dealing with the Coast Guard. He did have a hideaway apartment near Miami, however, where he sojourns in the sun.

The champion junketeer, according to the logs, has been Rep. Frank Clark (D-Pa.), who, as of June 1971, has used the Coast Guard planes no less than eleven times. Other multiple users, some for jaunts back to their home districts, included Reps. Silvio Conte (R-Mass.), Ed Garmatz (D-Md.), James Grover (R-N.Y.), and Walter Jones (D-N.C.).

The Coast Guard was just as ready to chauffeur Senators around the skies. Among those who received the VIP service were Senators Gordon Allott (R-Colo.), Caleb Boggs (R-Del.), Norris Cotton (R-N.H.), Robert Griffin (R-Mich.), Russell Long (D-La.), Ed Muskie (D-Me.), William Spong (D-Va.), John Stennis (D-Miss.), and Strom Thurmond (R-S.C.).

When Volpe isn't using the luxury jetliner himself, he may lend it to his fellow cabinet members. Commerce Secretary Maurice Stans, for example, used the Coast Guard executive plane to fly on a work-play junket to Latin America and Jamacia. The taxpayers were stuck with a $20,000 transportation bill.

Two former members, former Interior Secretary Wally Hickel and former Treasury Secretary David Kennedy, were also flown around by the Coast Guard. Florida's former Governor Claude Kirk's name also appears on the flight logs. Once, the propjet was used to fly a container full of "lunar samples" to Groton, Conn.

The kicker: despite the wholesale pleasure junketing, the Coast Guard asked the White House for another luxury plane, explaining that the "existing executive aircraft are not able to fully provide the transportation necessary for official Coast Guard use." The White House quietly said "no."

DOUBLE STANDARD JUSTICE

There is another type of privilege granted Congressmen. It's a sort of buffer against legal actions. One of the strongest buffers was Attorney General John Mitchell, the passionless protector of law and order, who puts politics ahead of the law. Mitchell not only has dropped the income tax case against Senator Tom Dodd (D-Conn.), he also made a deal with him not to press the other criminal charges hanging over his head. The Senator, who died in 1971, had pledged his vote to Mitchell on key issues.

There is abundant documentary evidence that Dodd accepted money and gifts from industries being investigated by committees on which he served; that he took money and loans from people for whom he obtained or attempted to obtain official appointments; that he took money and gifts from people for whom he performed official services; that he interceded with the federal government for his private law clients; and that he charged the government for trips that were essentially vacations. In most of these instances, Dodd appeared to have violated federal law. The Senate Ethics Committee, always reluctant to investigate a member of its own inner circle, delicately declined to go into these cases, referring them instead to the Justice Department.

One specific charge was that Dodd had pocketed $8,000 in cash from the International Latex Corporation. In return for the money, he was supposed to seek a major ambassadorship for the board chairman, A. N. Spanel. The intrigue proceeded far enough for Spanel's Washington operative, Irving Ferman, to send Dodd a resume about Mrs. Spanel, which noted that she was "fluent in Italian and French." Mitchell later moved against International Latex on this issue, but as evidence of his deal with Dodd, the indictment, incredibly, didn't even mention Dodd by name. The Justice Department was content rather to accuse the company of paying off an unnamed Senator.

In contrast, Mitchell bore down hard on former Senator Dan Brewster (D-Md.), for allegedly accepting a bribe from Spiegel, Inc., a Chicago mail-order house. Brewster didn't pocket the money but treated it as a campaign contribution. Yet the Justice Department indicted both Brewster and Spiegel.

The essential difference in the two cases is that the pathetic Brewster, broken in both health and spirit, had lost his political power. But Dodd was a pivotal member of the powerful Senate Judiciary Committee, which oversees the activities of the Justice Department. Without him, the committee broke down to eight conservatives and eight liberals. Dodd had always played ball with Chairman James Eastland (D-Miss.) on such matters as internal security. But on other issues, Dodd's votes were more responsive to the liberal attitudes of the voters back in Connecticut. Dodd's vote was crucial to Mitchell, therefore, on close-fought issues. On two showdown roll calls in 1969, Dodd voted for the administration's antimissile system and voted inside the Judiciary Committee to confirm Judge Clement Haynsworth to the Supreme Court.

Dodd voted against Haynsworth on the Senate floor, however, after waiting to see how everyone else lined up. It isn't uncommon for key

Senators to withhold their votes on close issues until they are sure of the outcome. Not until Dodd knew his vote wouldn't be needed to save Haynsworth, did he join the 55-to-45 majority against confirmation. Significantly, Vice President Agnew left behind his tally sheet, showing how he had expected the vote to go. Among the yeas, nays and "doubtfuls," he had firmly marked Dodd in favor of Haynsworth — evidence that Dodd's vote would have been available if it had been needed.

Attorney General Mitchell, in throwing out Dodd's income tax case, overruled the Internal Revenue Service which had recommended criminal prosecution. Revenue agents spent more than a year unraveling Dodd's tangled finances. They found bank accounts and personal loans all the way from Los Angeles to the Bahamas. Their call for criminal prosecution not only was approved by both the regional and national IRS offices but also had the full support of Jon Newman, then the U.S. Attorney in Connecticut. However, President Johnson on the eve of his retirement appointed Richard Crane right out of Dodd's office as Newman's assistant. LBJ and Dodd were close personal friends and political allies. From the day Crane moved into the U.S. Attorney's office, he worked vigorously to get Dodd off the hook. His strong opposition to criminal prosecution may have had some effect on the Justice Department. But the final decision to drop all criminal charges was made by Mitchell essentially for political reasons.

To show that this sort of political privilege granted Congressmen is general practice rather than a here-and-there whim of the Justice Department, we can turn to a page one story in the July 5, 1971, issue of *The Washington Post*. The story, broken by Post staff writer John Hanrahan, told how the Justice Department in early 1971 had blocked federal prosecutors in Baltimore from informing a grand jury that a Brooklyn congressman had conspired with a reputed organized crime leader to defraud the government on a $2 million Post Office mail truck leasing contract.

The writer reported that "high-ranking officials of the Justice Department's Criminal Division ordered George Beall, U.S. attorney for Maryland, to drop an investigation of Rep. Frank J. Brasco, D-N.Y., who was then serving his third term in office."

The case was dropped partly because the department felt there was no evidence that the alleged conspiracy bore fruit. Another factor in the decision, the news story stated, "was that the Justice Department told Beall it was concerned about unfavorable publicity it has been receiving for its use of conspiracy indictments against social and political militants and was reluctant to prosecute any further conspiracy cases." Rep. Brasco subsequently denied any impropriety or wrongdoing and said he was unaware of the investigation.

Government sources said that the Congressman was being investigated by the FBI and Beall's office in connection with allegations that Brasco conspired in 1968 with officials of the ANR Leasing Co. of New York to obtain renewal of a truck lease contract which ANR had with the Post Office Department in the New York area. The ANR firm reportedly was controlled by John ("Gentleman John") Masiello, 51, who is tagged by both New York and federal law officers as a member of the Mafia family headed by Vito Genovese. Masiello had been convicted in February, 1970, of charges of bribing postal officials in another case. The story was that Rep. Brasco had agreed to use his influence as a member of Congress and of the House Post Office and Civil Service Committee to assist ANR. In return for this, it was alleged, he was to receive a fee of perhaps $25,000.

THE OTHER SIDE OF THE COIN

The immunity of Congress goes only so far. Not all government agencies and agents are gun-shy of Congressional poppings. Stephen Sachs, for one, isn't. Wasn't. Sachs, the former U.S. attorney who investigated some of the biggest nabobs on Capitol Hill, has acknowledged behind closed doors that he freely subpoenaed the telephone records of members of Congress.

His grand jury investigations in Baltimore involved such headline figures as former Speaker John McCormack, House Majority Leader Hale Boggs, Sen. Russell Long (D-La), Sen. Vance Hartke (D-Ind.), former Rep. Arnold Olsen (D-Mont.), former Rep. James Morrison (D-La.), and former Sen. Dan Brewster (D-Md.). Of the lot, the grand jury indicted only Brewster on bribery charges that were later dismissed. But Sachs's hot breath on the backs of some prominent congressional necks has not endeared him to the powers on Capitol Hill.

Now a practising attorney in Baltimore, Sachs was hauled behind closed doors by the House Administration Committee to determine whether congressional rights had been violated.

"You have subpoenaed Congressmen's telephone records. Is that right?" demanded Chairman Wayne Hays, D-Ohio.

"Yes, sir," said Sachs.

"Did they know they were being subpoenaed?" pressed Hays. "Did the Congressmen know?"

"I doubt it very much," said Sachs. "Put it this way, I don't believe in any case they were informed officially."

"Did you ever have any knowledge of any subpoenas being issued for congressional telephone records where there was no allegation or suggestion of wrongdoing, just what a layman might call a fishing expedition?" asked the chairman.

"No, sir. . ." replied Sachs. "In no case was any subpoena issued by my office idly or maliciously or for any other reason than for good cause."

"You and other district attorneys," snorted Hays, "can subpoena almost any record of a Congressman, certainly their telephone records, which you have done. If I want to subpoena your records. . .or if I want a list of (State Department) phone calls, there is no way on God's earth I can do it, because the executive branch stands on executive privilege and refuses to surrender.... The legislative branch is at considerable disadvantage under the (separation-of-powers) theory when our records can be subpoenaed willy-nilly, but we cannot get our hand on any records we may want. . . ."

"In my firm judgment," Sachs replied, "the records of the phone company are the records of the phone company and not the records of the Congress."

But Hays would not be put off.

"The thing that bothers me," he snorted, "is that you can go in and grab a Member's records, and he may not know about it for six months or six years or maybe never."

"That is right," agreed Sachs.

"Do you feel from your vast experience in the Justice Department," interrupted Rep. Sam Devine, R-Ohio, "that Members of Congress are entitled to any treatment any different from any ordinary citizen in connection with their business telephone or home telephone records?"

"No, Congressman," said Sachs, "quite frankly I do not." He pointed out that the corruption statutes include Members of Congress as "public officials." "It is the Congress which has made Members of the Congress amenable to the Criminal Code," he said.

"How can you in Baltimore issue a subpoena," demanded Rep. William Dickinson, R-Ala., "to the (telephone) company of the District of Columbia?"

"Because in a criminal case there is nationwide service of process. . . ," explained Sachs. "The U.S. attorney or a grand jury can issue subpoenas to any place in the United States."

"What if you wanted the records of the White House?" asked Dickinson. "Can you get them from the telephone company by just subpoenaeing them?"

"I never tried," said the former U.S. attorney. "I don't know."

Grumped Rep. Fred Schwengel, R-Iowa: "I am impressed with the obvious unfairness that prevails between a Member of Congress and the Executive.... It seems to me we do not have a co-equal situation when the Executive has certain powers and rights in carrying out their mission, and we in Congress do not."

NIXON TO THE ATTACK

If Congressmen are vulnerable to a few investigators, they are doubly vulnerable to the machinations of their colleagues in politics. For politics, let the word go out, is a ruthless game. The story of Speaker McCormack and President Nixon will serve to illustrate.

During John McCormack's last days as Speaker, President Nixon honored the old man to his face but tried behind his back to pin criminal charges on him. The President, hailing McCormack's half century of public service, presented him with a plaque at a White House luncheon. Not long afterward, the President invited McCormack to the White House for a private breakfast and promised to continue to consult him after his retirement. Yet all the while, the Nixon administration was digging quietly into McCormack's activities in search of skulduggery. Friends of his were hauled before a federal grand jury in New York City for secret questioning about their relationship with the retiring Speaker. They were notified ominously that the grand jury was investigating "the Speaker's office." Then they were asked whether they had ever given McCormack any money or gifts.

Three of the old man's close friends were invited to the White House luncheon, then subpoenaed before the secret grand jury within a few days. They were Rubin Epstein, president of Boston's City Bank and Trust; George Feldman, former Ambassador to Malta and Luxembourg; and Peter Cloherty, consultant for a Boston engineering firm. Epstein was called before the grand jury three times. The same questions were repeated at each appearance. He testified that he had never given McCormack anything except, perhaps, a box of cigars at Christmas time. The records of the bank's dealings with McCormack were also subpoenaed, revealing only that the Speaker kept a modest savings account at City Bank and Trust. Feldman was asked, also in vain, whether he had paid McCormack for recommending him as an Ambassador. The same line of questioning was started on Cloherty whose firm, McGuire Associates, was ordered to produce all papers relating to federal contracts. "We would need a freight car," grumbled Cloherty.

In 1969, a reporter, posing as a student intern, stayed for two weeks in McCormack's office working with and observing his aide, Martin Sweig. In that time he dug up enough evidence to write that Sweig, using McCormack's name and sometimes imitating his voice, had fixed federal cases for a five percenter named Nathan Voloshen. McCormack got advance word of the column and suspended Sweig the day before its release date. Sweig was subsequently convicted of perjury in connection with the fixes.

A long investigation found that McCormack, a product of South

Boston's "Last Hurrah" politics, would happily fix anything from a traffic ticket to a government contract for his friends, but turned up absolutely no evidence that the old man had ever pocketed a penny for his political favors. From competent sources, it was learned that his personal fortune was little more than $100,000. For a man who has spent 33 years in politics, this is persuasive evidence of his honesty.

Like most Congressmen, McCormack practiced law out of the back door of his congressional office until he was appointed to the House Ways and Means Committee in 1930. Then he decided too many of his clients had an interest in the money matters before the committee. To avoid a conflict, he quietly closed his law office and began to live on his government salary. He always kept his personal and congressional accounts strictly separate. He carefully segregated his mail and telephone calls, for example, paying for all personal postage and calls himself. He routinely turned down compaign contributions, since he had almost no campaign expenses. Occasionally, he would take donations for political friends. But he kept a scrupulous record of how the money was distributed. Careless as "Old Jawn" may have been about some associates, it may be that investigation has shown that he is, at heart, an old-fashioned puritan governed by a strong Catholic conscience.

CONGRESSIONAL ETHICS

When the AFL and CIO merged in 1955, one of the Federation's first acts was to establish an ethical practices committee. A year later, chairman Al Hayes received a tongue-in-cheek telegram from the old labor lion, John L. Lewis. "Have you found any ethical practices?" it read.

The same question should be addressed to Congress. After 175 years of corruption and conflicts on Capitol Hill, the Senate (in 1964) and the House (1966) finally formed committees on ethics. It was the least Congress could do after the Bobby Baker, Adam Clayton Powell and Tom Dodd scandals. "Least" is the right word. The committees have shown more interest in concealing than exposing unethical practices on the Hill. The prevailing codes of ethics contain more loopholes than limitations. The result is that Congressional chicanery has continued unabated and has become more devious.

A clue to the congressional attitude toward unethical conduct can be found in the Senate Ethics Committee's initial report. "The Senate must not only be free from improper influences," wrote the committee, "but must also be, like Caesar's wife, free from the appearance of impropriety." The emphasis has been on appearance rather than actual impropriety.

The committee's quietly capable chief counsel, Benjamin Fern, admits the ethics panel does "a lot of nipping in the bud." The real aim is to identify and isolate Senate misconduct before the public finds out about it. The wrongdoing may be corrected or condoned, but the main effort is to cover it up.

The Senate requires its members, for example, to file a detailed financial report. This is supposed to include copies of their tax returns, lists of their legal fees over $1,000, names of corporations that retain them as officers or directors, an inventory of their property in excess of $10,000 value, all trusts in which they have an interest, all liabilities over $5,000, and the source and value of all gifts. The report is then placed in a sealed envelope and turned over to the Comptroller General, never to be seen again except in the unlikely event a Senator is investigated by the Ethics Committee.

Congress also ignores a lot of unethical practices by never defining them. Explained John Swanner, the easy-going staff director of the House Ethics Committee, with a shrug; "Is a Congressman answerable to the House or to his constituents? At what point does an outside activity become a conflict of interest? What is a conflict, anyway? The courts have never said. Who is responsible for remedies—the people, the body or the law? These are touchy questions, and they don't yield to simplicity."

Certainly, the answers can't be found in the ethics codes which leave enough loopholes for each member pretty much to set his own ethical standards. Take Emanuel Celler, the 83-year-old House Judiciary chairman, who apparently has never seen anything unethical about a double-door legal practice. The law prohibits a Congressman from handling clients with matters before the federal government. Celler and his partners got around that by using two doors to their law office. One has Celler's name on it; the other does not. Both firms share the same furniture, fixtures and telephones. Clients with federal business go through the non-Celler door.

The most flagrant weakness in the codes and the major cause of congressional malfeasance is campaign financing. The House ethics code completely dismisses the subject, leaving it to be taken up "by the appropriate legislative committee." The Senate code requires disclosure of "contributions" but leaves convenient loopholes.

Conflicts of interest literally flourish on the Hill under the regulations now in force. The worst conflicts can be lumped into three broad categories:

1. *Business and Investments.* Both Houses are populated by men who legislate and regulate businesses which they themselves own, run, or invest in.

The big conflicts of interest involve financial institutions. At least 97

House members in the 91st Congress had ties with banks, savings and loan associations, and other financial firms. Over 40 were officers or directors. A dozen bankers actually served on the House Banking Committee. Nine members of this committee accepted reduced-rate loans from the National Bank of Washington. All told, 124 Congressmen received similar bank loans at 3 per cent less interest than available to less blessed citizens.

The Senate's most unabashed lawmaker-businessman is Sen. Russell Long (D-La.), whose father founded the Win-or-Lose oil company in the early 1930's. Happily the company won more than it lost. Disbanded in 1938 for a tax advantage, Win-or-Lose was later quietly reorganized as a family partnership. Today the business largely handles the rent paid by big oil firms for the privilege of drilling on Long land. As Senate Finance chairman, Long cheerfully confesses to an "identity of interests" with oilmen and takes pains to see that the industry gets every possible tax break.

2. *Law Firms.* In a study published in 1970, the New York City Bar Association concluded that "law practices have played a disproportionate role in the history of congressional scandals." Indeed, most of the major scandals of recent years have involved law firms in one way or another. Bobby Baker used his firm to channel payoffs from lobbyists to legislators; Senator Dodd collected law fees in payment for his many "services"; and former Sen. Ed Long (D-Mo.) was accused of accepting "referral fees" as payments for helping the imprisoned Teamsters president, James Hoffa.

Like Celler, many Congressmen operate "double-doors" arrangements to evade the law. Almost all the legislator-lawyers represent business firms, and it is difficult to conceive of a business today which is free of involvement with Uncle Sam.

3. *Honorariums.* The Senate has a fairly strict rule requiring that honorariums at least be disclosed. While many such fees are legitimate, they frequently serve as conduits for special interest groups. The Seafarer's Union, while under Justice Department investigation, paid $1,000 each to three Senators in 1969, $500 to another. The American Medical Association frequently doles out large sums to hear speeches by Senators who agree with its views.

An uproar was heard in 1963 when one of the authors of this book (Jack Anderson) published in his syndicated column a report on Congressmen who cheat. He was challenged to appear before a congressional committee to back up the charges. He prepared testimony which included the names of Bobby Baker and Adam Clayton Powell. But on the appointed day, the committee backed down and refused to listen to his testimony. The Baker and Powell scandals—and later the Dodd case—had to be blown up in the press before Congress would investigate. Out of these investigations eventually came the codes and committees that were supposed to regulate ethics on Capitol Hill.

Eight years after the first revelations, have the ethics of Congressmen improved? Here are the authors' conclusions:

1. The standards of conduct simply aren't enforced, and there is evidence they were never meant to be. Congress is a cozy club which holds that its foremost duty is to protect its image. The mere act of forming ethics committees was considered sufficient obeisance to the clamor for reform. The attitude toward offenders, therefore, is one of benign tolerance.

2. The rules of conduct are written in such broad and vague terms that few Congressmen, including those who serve on the ethics committees, seem to know exactly what is unethical. The House Ethics Committee, in particular, seems to be still in the throes of defining its functions.

3. Both houses supposedly prevent conflicts by requiring "financial disclosure." The theory is that informed voters can decide for themselves whether their Congressman has compromised the public trust for private gain. But the briefest examination exposes the financial disclosure rules as utter sham.

For 182 years, the American people have tolerated congressional chiseling. It will take a louder clamor from the public—in the form of letters now and ballots every other November—before corruption is brought under control.

LOBBYISTS

DOMESTIC

The delicate art of influencing legislation popularly known as lobbying, named for the Capitol lobbies where the backstage persuasion often occurs, has moved a great distance from the days when votes were bought with black satchels full of money and nights on the town with painted ladies. The methods have become refined since the 19th Century railroad mogul, Collis Huntington, wrote his three Southern Pacific partners that it would cost only $200,000 to highball a pet bill through Congress. "This coming session," he explained, "will be composed of the hungriest set of men that ever got together."

Today's successful lobbyists are more likely to be smooth professionals, skilled in the soft sell. They seldom engage in blatant currying of favor. Well tailored and turned out, they make their pitches subtly over martinis at the posh Metropolitan Club or over golf balls at the exclusive Burning Tree course. But they can also retain a Senator's law firm or deliver cash in a paper sack to those who prefer that sort of gross transaction.

If lobbying techniques have grown sophisticated, the name of the game is still the same: special interest. Lobbyists may call themselves legislative counsels or Washington representatives. They may organize write-your-Congressman pitches and spend their money on selective campaign contributions instead of outright bribes. They may discourse at length on the valuable services they provide to overworked Congressmen who would not be able to vote intelligently on complicated bills without their expertise. But they are still hired, in the final analysis, to sell their clients' special interests.

The lobbyists' role in government, to hear them tell it, is sorely misunderstood. They merely exercise their Constitutional right of petition, albeit with special vigor. The First Amendment guarantees "the right of the people peaceably to assemble, and to petition the Government for a redress of grievances." Apparently the founding fathers did not foresee that professional petitioners would bring such heavy axes to grind.

Although a 1946 law requires all lobbyists to register and to give yearly reports of their spending, the most effective lobbyists seldom do. They may be lawyers who devote most of their time to guiding corporations through the trackless wastes of government, or corporate "Washington reps" who merely follow the progress of special bills. When a little pressure is needed, they will point out the Senators and bring big names from their home states to make the personal contacts.

There are intelligent men in Washington who are convinced that lobbyists actually exercise very little power, because opposing lobbies cancel each other out on major issues, leaving the public interest as the determining factor. It is true that lobbyists come from all spectra of the American scene; they represent industries, unions, farm organizations, veterans groups, trade associations. When Big Labor clashes with Big Business, they may indeed produce a stalemate. But this would hardly be true of tax reforms, for instance, because every group lobbies for its own tax loophole unmindful of the others. The evidence is more persuasive that legislation is shaped as much by the hidden influences as by the public debates. These less visible forces are constantly applied by lawyers and lobbyists, expediters who are dedicated to the proposition that the national interest is identical with their particular interest. They do not like to call themselves lobbyists. "It just isn't sophisticated to call yourself a lobbyist in Washington any more," explained Dale Miller, one of the most successful what-cha-ma-call-its in Washington.

Certainly, the effective operators no longer hang around the Capitol lobbies. They remain above the battle, cool, convivial, and, if possible, invisible.

BANK PRESSURE

Congressmen always shut the doors and bar the press when they want to hide their activities from the folks back home. Members of the House Banking Committee, therefore, took pains last fall to keep their discussions of the banking lobby secret. They didn't want the voters to know how slavishly they had defended the banks whose earnings in 1969 were the fattest in history. These record profits were squeezed out of the public, as interest rates soared in sudden great bursts like a multistage rocket.

The banks are not as beloved by the voters, therefore, as by certain Congressmen who have accepted cut-rate loans, legal fees, campaign contributions and other financial benefits from bankers in return for legislative favors. Confidential loan records made available to the authors, for example, reveal that last year 124 House members were in hock to the staid National Bank of Washington. They were able to borrow the money at 6½ per cent interest at a time when all other borrowers were paying at least 8 per cent.

It is scarcely surprising, therefore, that House Banking Chairman Wright Patman (D-Tex.) ran into opposition when he tried to curb the influence of the banks on Capitol Hill. Looking every bit as benign as the bankers he battles, Patman ordered an investigation of the banking lobby. He was stopped cold by his own committee members who countermanded his orders to the staff investigators. Patman subsequently took his case to the public in a speech to the National Press Club. Then behind closed doors, he tried again to persuade his committee to authorize the investigation.

News media obtained a copy of the secret transcript of that session which illustrates the bullwhip power of the banking lobby. Congressman after Congressman argued heatedly against a bank probe. The transcript shows that committee members pounced unmercifully upon their chairman for seeking an investigation. They angrily demanded the specific evidence from him that they had blocked the staff from digging up.

Rep. Bill Brock (R-Tenn.), who owned stock in the Hamilton National Bank of Chattanooga and Nashville, led the attack. He rapped Patman for making "the kind of allegations he has made against what he calls the banking lobby but which directly imply wrongdoing on the part of members of this committee . . . . "I think it is doggone well time that this committee acted to substantiate whatever charges have been made. And if there is no substantiation, I think an apology is due the entire committee."

The chairman, his benign smile unchanged, started to present his case but Rep. Garry Brown (R-Mich.) interrupted.

"Do you think you ought to be sworn if you are going to testify?" he demanded. The suggestion that a chairman be put under oath by his own committee was insulting, but Patman ignored it.

"No," he said mildly, "I don't need to be sworn."

Then he ticked off his reasons for seeking an investigation of the banking lobby. "The banking industry today," he said, "represents about $700 billion in assets which is multiplied by its vast powers to control the nation's credit. Regardless of one's feelings about this industry, its potential to influence public opinion and public decisions is obvious."

He claimed that high interest rates are feeding the fires of inflation like gasoline. The combination of tight credit and steep costs, he warned, had started the nation on the downslide to depression. It is imperative to counteract the influence of the bankers, he argued, and to reverse the government's tight money policy. To perpetuate their influence, Patman charged, the banks raise an annual $535 million kitty.

"They have as much as $1 million for every member of Congress," he said, "not for them personally, but they have a fund every year that would be equal to this. I want to make it plain that I am not impeaching a member of Congress on this, but they have over $535 million to spend."

Rep. Tom Ashley (D-Ohio), whose former legislative assistant Kathleen Lucey was the sister of a bank lobbyist, snapped, "If you say that no banking legislation is passed other than as a result of the economic power of the banks, I say you are a liar."

Patman described how the banking lobby had been snooping into the private lives of Congressmen. He had been furnished a copy of a questionnaire, he said, "distributed by a banking organization and designed to gather the most intimate details of a Congressmen's private life. The questionnaire seeks information on the Congressman's drinking habits. It inquires as to whether he is a 'customer' of a bank . . . . It asks about his family."

But it was Patman, not the bankers, who continued to draw the committee members' ire. Rep. Robert Stephens, Jr. (D-Ga.), then a stockholder in the First National Bank of Athens, Ga., accused the chairman of pressing for the bank lobby probe out of vindictiveness over the defeat of his one-bank holding company bill. This would have prevented banks from going into competition with their own customers.

"This investigation is sought," snorted Stephens, "because you lost one-bank holding company bill that you wanted."

"You would question the integrity of this committee as a means toward your end," agreed Rep. Seymour Halpern (R-N.Y.), who had wangled over $100,000 in easy loans from a wide assortment of banks in New York, Florida, and points in between. Both Halpern and Stephens had received cut-rate loans from the National Bank of Washington.

"The chairman's statement before the Press Club," broke in Brock fiercely, "was the most irresponsible, venomous, vengeful attack I have ever witnessed by a member of this body on other members of this body."

"Oh no," protested Patman, "not on other members."

"If you are going to investigate lobbying," declared Brock, cutting Patman off, "you have got to talk about all kinds of influence. You have got to talk about oil paintings. You have got to talk about paid trips—weekends. There are a lot of ways of effecting or maintaining relationships with a member of Congress."

Patman happily cited other ways that are used to woo members of Congress. He quoted former Sen. Frank Lausche (D-Ohio), who had written to him about the lobby investigation. Lausche had told in his letter, according to Patman, how banks influence legislators "one, by buying insurance policies from those legislators; two, hiring those legislators as real estate appraisers; three, hiring those legislators to act as legal counsel in the bank's business."

It was Stephens who offered the formal motion to kill Patman's proposed probe. The motion passed by a 19-13 vote.

"I consider that I have been defeated, that you voted against the lobby (investigation)," said Patman. He was no longer smiling.

THE LADIES' LOBBY

The ladies' lobby, in questioning the manhood of deer hunters, drew enraged howls from the firearms lobby. The battle of the lobbies began when the Friends of Animals, led by nine famous and beautiful women, protested turning deer hunters loose in New Jersey's Great Swamp National Wildlife Refuge to reduce the herd.

The lovely ladies, including Lauren Bacall, Ali MacGraw, Patrice Munsel and June Havoc, accused the hunters of slaughtering deer to prove their own virility because they fail "on better proving grounds (like) a boudoir."

"We're not turned on by a show of masculinity which takes place in the forest through maiming or occasionally killing helpless animals," mocked the ladies in handbills. "Hunter, make it dear, not deer. Will you? Won't you? Can't you?"

Cut to the quick, the Firearms Lobby of America issued its own handbills assailing the "female show business personalities." These audacious females had compared "hunters to the infamous perverted Marquis de Sade," whined the firearms lobby.

The gals' plea that hunters prove their "virility (in) a boudoir," instead of by killing deer, was branded as "the most diabolical (scheme) of all." The firearms fighters called for contributions to do battle against the ladies' ideas, not in the fields nor the bedrooms, but in the courts.

The Women's Liberation Movement, incidentally has the best underground in Washington. Women in government — secretaries, clerks and executives alike — pass all they hear along the women's grapevine. The word is whispered from coast to coast over official, toll-free telephone lines. Feminist newsletters like *Spokeswoman, Women Today,* and *The Activist* further spread the word. President Nixon's off-hand comments, for example, are fed into the grapevine. Within days, every feminist in the country knows what the president said about women. Here are just a few items we have picked up from the women's underground:

● In public, President Nixon professes to be a champion of equality for women. But in private, he would like all women to be domesticated like his wife and daughters.

● Senator Birch Bayh is supposed to be women's best friend on Capitol Hill. But Bayh and his boys have been heard to make disparaging remarks about feminists, and the word is spreading that the senator is a phony.

● Spies at the Civil Service Commission have frequently reported the derogatory remarks of Chairman Robert Hampton. He is now on the feminist blacklist.

Senators, representatives and government officials have women on their staffs who are part of the underground. Women right in the White House belong to the feminist movement. They try to convert the men they work for, and they spread the word about the unreconstructed. As one feminist told us with a confident wink: "We know who is for us and who is agin us." At a recent meeting of cabinet wives, Presdent Nixon asked the women to become his secret agents and spread the word about his programs. What he didn't realize was that secret agents are already spreading the word about Nixon. Some of them were eavesdropping on his meeting.

SCHOOL CRUSADE

The once fuddy-duddy National Education Association prepared a scathing attack on the federal budget crew for spending $10,000 to train and equip each soldier, but only $839 per student. The NEA, headed by a tough former Nashville school marm, Helen Bain, quietly produced tapes for shipment to 6,000 radio stations. These ought to outrage some of the nation's 2.3 million teachers. A typical tape opens with the sneering voice of a White House budget maker:

"... one C-5A transport $47 million ..."

A second voice asks, "What uh ... What are you doing?"

Voice 1: "Figuring out the federal budget. Who are you?"

Voice 2: "Just a taxpayer."

Voice 1:   "All right. Let's see... where was I? Total military budget—67 billion, aid to public schools about 4 and 6/10th billion..."

Voice 2: "Wait a minute. You're spending 14 times more for the military than for education. Isn't somebody gonna get wise?"

Voice 1: "Not on that kinda money, they're not."

Mrs. Bain, an attractive blonde, has told intimates that the traditional schoolteachers' hat-in-hand approach to the White House has brought school kids little more than shabby schools and coverless books. Meanwhile the Pentagon has been wallowing in wasteful projects.

2013020

"...IT WORKS THIS WAY..."

The top echelon of Washington's special pleaders play all sides and all the angles of the federal triangle—5,000 registered and unregistered lobbyists who practice the art of gentle persuasion. They have learned that it is more effective to massage egos than to twist arms. They seek to ingratiate themselves with legislators, in subtle ways that put legislators in their debt.

To further these friendships, the influence merchants eagerly provide small favors—theater tickets, imported liquors, French perfumes, free transportation; nothing so gross that the legislators could be accused of being bribed. It is the accumulation, rather than any single gift, that gradually obligates them. They can ride in style to the Kentucky Derby in the American Railroad Association's special train or take a cruise down the Potomac in the Freight Forwarders' air-conditioned yacht.

Some pressure groups keep hospitality suites near Capitol Hill where Congressmen can find relaxation from the legislative grind over a short snort, a long cigar, and, perhaps, a friendly game of poker. One poker session used to convene regularly in gold-papered Suite 512 of the Congressional Hotel, situated conveniently across the street from the House Office Buildings. The suite was maintained by a number of cooperating lobbyists, headed by S&H Green Stamps' Robert Oliver and the Hod Carriers' Jack Curran. Across the poker chips they may have scored an occasional point for their clients, but both Oliver and Curran have denied the base rumor that the Congressmen almost always won the big pots.

Many lobbyists keep files on the backgrounds, interest, and weaknesses of the Congressmen with whom they deal. These files are frequently more detailed — and far more fascinating — than those kept by Washington's political reporters. If a lobbyist knows that a key Congressman has a weakness for liquor, or girls, or cash in an envelope, the approach can be quick and painless.

The best way for lobbyists to show their appreciation for a Congressman, of course, is to contribute to his campaign. And the plunk of every donated coin adds emphasis to the need for reform on the greatest evil of the American political system. For most Congressional campaigns have become financed mainly by the special interests and pressure groups. The sad truth is that the American voter often cannot be bothered to go to the polls, let alone give money. Even the most honest Congressman cannot entirely escape doing business with the special interests. Those candidates who have tried to finance campaigns from small contributions have learned quickly that the fat cats are indispensable. Indeed, it is a miracle of politics and a tribute to officeholders that the pressure groups do not wield more influence than they do.

Probably no lobby in the country is more determined than the American Medical Association, that staunch defender of the status quo. Anything that might bring about any change, no matter how slight, is diagnosed darkly as "socialized medicine" — the worst ailment the AMA can imagine. The AMA stimulates doctors all over the country to bring political pressure to bear on their congressmen, an effective technique since the legislators look upon doctors and ministers as pillars of society and, therefore, leaders of thought in their communities.

Under the law, the AMA cannot engage openly in politics and still retain its tax-exempt status. The doctors got around that by forming a political arm called the American Political Action Committee, which they took pains to disguise as an independent body. Yet the AMA not only formed the new organization but selected the doctor-directors who run it. When the records of congressional candidates are reviewed to determine who should get the doctors' support, AMA and AMPAC participate together in the screening process. First call upon AMPAC's treasury usually goes to the House Ways and Means members who battled faithfully against medicare. But anyone who will stand four square against "socialized medicine" can count on a donation from the doctors.

The AMPAC dumped an estimated $3 million into the political kitty in 1962, though the exact amount can be only estimated. It is known, for instance, that Alabama's 2,240 doctors donated $33,000 to the national fund though not a cent of this was spent in Alabama. They kicked in far more money to their own local candidates.

Because of a series of news stories about these AMPAC activities in 1962, the doctors took extra pains to conceal whom they supported and how much they spent in the 1964-70 campaigns. It is evident, however, that they passed out even more in their last great stand against medicare. Ignoring such issues as the Vietnam war, the doctors crowded aboard Barry Goldwater's bandwagon and kept on beating the medicare drum as they went down gloriously to defeat. They mounted an organized letter-writing campaign against other pro-medicare candidates, calling these unenlightened souls "enemies of private enterprise" and "advocates of socialism." An instruction sheet to Ohio doctors cautioned: "Secretaries and doctors should address their envelopes and sign the letters now and hold them for mailing the week before election. . . . Add a P.S. in ink to make the letter more personal."

The doctors were so obsessed over medicare that they entered into a weird lobbying alliance with the cigarette makers. Anticipating the Surgeon General's report on smoking and health, the tobacco men sought to counteract it. They offered to finance a new AMA study of the smoking hazard, thus hoping to give the impression that the government report wasn't conclusive and that smokers need not kick the habit until the AMA results came in at some indefinite date. In return, the tobacco lobbyists promised to use their influence in Congress to block the medicare bill. The doctors were more concerned about medicare, which they fancied to be a threat to their fees, than about the threat to the nation's lungs. So it happened that those who cause and those who cure lung trouble lay down together in millennial bliss.

FOREIGN

At last count by the Attorney General's office, there are 453 registered and active foreign agents in the United States. Registered foreign agents differ from unregistered foreign agents in at least two notable ways. First, they are not here, ostensibly, to steal state secrets. Second, they are not foreign — or most of them are not. Instead they are American citizens retained by foreign governments and industrial interests for the purpose of prevailing upon the U.S. government to act with kindness toward their clients. And sometimes that kindness is translated into economic advantage for the client nation or company, which, in all likelihood and for a substantial fee, will then continue to engage the services of its favorite registered foreign agent in Washington.

The typical foreign agent, then, is a variation on the legendary domestic lobbyist. Instead of promoting a special sector or interest or facet of the American political kaleidoscope, he pitches for a foreign power or enterprise, whose call on the American government is likely to be even less legitimate and open to even more suspicion than the hardly ennobling entreaties of the home-grown variety of pitchman. Which is another way of saying that what the foreign lobbyist seeks for his client may not coincide with the interests of the American people.

A major part of the lobbying effort by foreign agents is aimed, naturally enough, at Congress, with its tight hold on the federal purse. On Congress, therefore, falls a large part of the obligation to screen out the legitimate pleas of foreign agents from the mass of blatantly self-serving requests. But an unsettling number of Congressmen have, over the years, been responsive to overtures — and campaign contributions — from foreign agents whose missions have better served their clients' interests than those of the people who elected the Congress.

No foreign agent has represented his clients in Washington with more single-minded zeal than a stubby, Chicago-born public relations man named Julius Klein — Major General (Ret.) Julius Klein — now in his late sixties and living in retirement. If, in the ceaseless pursuit of his clients' interests, he also fattened his own bank account, no one can accuse him of sinning — only of the most brazenly self-serving and insensitive effort of modern times to curry congressional favor. He was at least a part of the heavy burden that dragged the late Senator Thomas J. Dodd of Connecticut into the prize seat before the Senate Select Committee on Standards and Ethics which convened in 1966 to take a look at the Senator's affairs and wound up censuring him.

But even earlier than that, in 1963, the Senate Foreign Relations Committee, under Senator Fulbright's chairmanship, was reviewing the activities of nondiplomatic representatives of foreign powers in the United States, and singled Klein out for special attention. It cited him as an example of a public relations practitioner who "by exaggeration or misuse of his relationships with members of Congress can for his own purposes create for foreign governments, officials or business interests a mistaken and sometimes unflattering picture of how our governmental institutions function." The committee was referring mainly to the curious correspondence between Dodd and Klein, a correspondence that over the years drew a picture of a PR man barking orders, and a U.S. Senator jumping through hoops.

On September 4, 1959, for example, Klein sent the Senator a "Dear Tom" letter, virtually demanding that he deliver a eulogy to West German Chancellor Konrad Adenauer. A fulsome speech, written by Harry Blake of the Klein Public Relations Inc.'s staff, was helpfully enclosed. "As soon as you have edited the copy," Klein instructed the Senator, "please deliver it and have Jack Fleischer (Dodd's press man) release it, not only to the American press, but also the German correspondents accredited to the National Press Corps, and send a copy over to the press attache of the German Embassy, including Minister Krapf, so that this will get the widest circulation in Europe." (Klein was the Washington representative for several German companies and organizations including the Cologne Society for the Protection of Post World War II Investments and the Society for German-American

Cooperation out of Wiesbaden. The latter paid him a fat fee of $150,000 a year for activities that never have been made clear.)

Nor did Klein, when dissatisfied, hesitate to rap the Senator's knuckles. In 1961, for instance, Dodd wrote President Kennedy that Klein was just the man to fill an opening on the American Battle Monuments Commission. "I believe you could not make a finer appointment," Dodd wrote, "because General Klein has indeed distinguished himself as an outstanding military man." Klein was pleased over such a warm endorsement. But the post, alas, went to another, and Julius was back at Dodd's door for the next honor that came around, a spot on the U.S. Advisory Commission on Information. "I am sure you will want to add your endorsement," Klein wrote Dodd on July 14, 1962. "But what is more important, couldn't you take this up personally with President Kennedy and with Lyndon Johnson so that we not lose this opportunity by default, as happened last time?"

Dodd dutifully fired off a letter to President Kennedy and received a bare acknowledgment from Lawrence F. O'Brien, then a White House aide. Again, the post was given to another. Disappointed, Klein wrote bitterly to Dodd, "You know, Tom, friendship is a two-way street. I don't blame you for what happened, but what I am more disappointed in is that I didn't hear from you at all, either way. I am confident that had I been in your place and the roles had been reversed, I would have been in constant touch with you." This got Dodd's hackles up, and he fired back a testy reply "I did what I said I would do, but I am sure you will understand that I cannot guarantee any performance." Although still sulking, Klein would give the Senator another chance. He wrote, "Tom, I never expected you to guarantee any performance.... Anyhow this is water over the dam."

When Klein was about to lose his biggest German accounts, he demanded, in a rush of wires, letters and memos, that Senator Dodd go to Europe and assure a half dozen or so influential Germans that he, Klein, still had the ear and heart of the United States Congress. He even went so far as to write down, in note form, little laudatory remarks about Klein which the Senator was to mouth to each person on the schedule. And Dodd did it!

Although during the Senate Ethics Committee hearings Dodd denied he had gone to Europe on an errand for Klein, and certainly that he had received any instructions, it was established that Dodd, while in Germany allegedly on U.S. government business, saw most of the people whom Klein had asked him to see. And there is extant a letter dated April 21, 1964, written by Klein to Dodd a few days after Dodd had returned from his Europe trip. "I had a very nice letter from former Chancellor Adenauer (one of the names on Klein's list) and am very pleased." But Julius, hoping for some frosting on the cake, added, "I presume, Tom, you will write the various people you saw over there and if you do, I would appreciate it if you would add a PS: 'I was indeed glad to discuss with you also the fine work of our mutual good friend General Klein.'. . . . Once again, my thanks for your true friendship, and I am always ready to be of service to you in the interest of our country and good government."

The ethics committee chose to bring charges against Dodd on only two counts: converting campaign contributions to his private use and billing the government for travel expenses that were paid by private organizations. It recommended that he be censured by the Senate — and he duly was, by a 95-5 vote on the single charge of the campaign funds.

One final example of a foreign lobby at work against the best interests of the American taxpayer should be presented. Former Representative Harold Cooley, a touchy North Carolina Democrat, headed the House Agriculture Committee in 1965. When he was drafting the sugar legislation that year, he invited lobbyists Irving Hoff of the Cane Sugar Refiners and Phil Jones of the Beet Sugar Association to sit in at the committee sessions, despite the fact that the sessions were closed to the public and press. In the House Rules Committee, the next step toward passage of the bill, Cooley spoke up sharply for his scheme to report the sugar bill to the House floor under a rule barring amendments. This would have forced the opposition to settle for his bill or no bill at all. Representative Richard Bolling (D-Mo.) asked Cooley at the closed Rules Committee hearing why he had ignored the Agriculture Department's recommendations on the bill and had written his own instead.

"We didn't write this bill for the Agriculture Department," Cooley retorted. Bolling kept probing, and finally Cooley lost patience and snapped, "And we didn't write this bill for you."

Nobody ever found out for whom the bill had been written; certainly not for the taxpayers. Cooley's bill not only allowed more sugar into the country than the Agriculture Department wished, but also allocated the quotas to countries with the best political connections rather than the most need. Nevertheless, Rules Committee Chairman Howard Smith (D-Va.) sided with Cooley on the no-amendment rule and called for a show of hands. Six went up for the ayes; six for the nays — because John Young (D-Tex.) didn't vote. The bill went to the floor under the rule Cooley demanded, and it passed October 13, 1965, by a 348-147 margin. And that's what happens to the taxpayers' interests when they collide with the lobbies in the back rooms of Congress.

PRESIDENCY

"I pray Heaven to bestow the best of Blessings on this House and all that shall hereafter inhabit it. May none but honest and wise Men ever rule under this roof."

That was John Adams writing to his wife on his first night in the still unfinished White House. Through the years his wish has been running at about 50 per cent efficiency. That is to say, while generally honest men have inhabited the White House, not all of them have been burdened with wisdom. And even those who were blessed with brains often had trouble exercising them.

For a new President is handicapped with a mere four-year lease in which time he must kick and gouge a cumbersome Congress into action; not just any action, but action specifically affecting the President's pet programs. And if the obdurate Congress weren't enough, there is always the incredible bureaucratic labyrinth to be learned — a lesson that defies mastery, and so leaves each Chief Executive more or less at the mercy of the bureaucratic holdovers from past administrations.

Wisdom is not the ultimate quality a candidate for the presidency must have; it's nice if he does have it, perhaps even useful, but more important qualities are charisma, a good television image, heaps of campaign money, the solid backing of his party, and a large portion of very good luck. Wisdom? Well, that's really not a grabber among the voters these days. Ask any Madison Avenue ad man. It didn't noticeably help Adlai Stevenson in his two shots at Dwight Eisenhower in the 1950's. Some people think it may even have hurt him. To be called "egghead," remember, was a political slander in those days.

But "charisma" and "image," they're the qualities that make a President. The deciding difference between Nixon and Kennedy in 1960 is said, in fact, to have been JFK's charisma and Nixon's lack of it.

But Nixon fixed that. He took a store-bought "image" into his successful 1968 campaign against Hubert Humphrey. Joe McGinnis in his book *The Selling of the President* revealed in excruciating detail how presidential candidate Richard Nixon was marketed to the American public in 1968 like a bottle of bubble bath.

Today the program for selling the President is far more comprehensive than the one that brought him into office. Richard Nixon the candidate lacked power. Richard Nixon the President has at his disposal the full weight of the federal government. Where Nixon's image makers could control only the message in 1968, they seek control of the media in 1972.

The Washington press corps is kept comfortable but kept in the dark. Nixon, convinced he could not win over the Eastern Establishment newspapers, wrote them off the day he took office. He didn't antagonize reporters; he was as amenable to them as he could bring himself to be. But according to his grand strategy, he doesn't need their support, and he regularly goes over their heads. When he has a point to put across, he goes directly to the people, usually by using television. No President has ever made more use of the magic picture box. Press conferences are studiously staged to the President's advantage. Televised interviews and "conversations" are carefully planned.

President Nixon hugely enjoys the drama of interrupting all network television programs with some electrifying announcement. But this method of government-by-surprise is causing havoc with the orderly procedures. Critics are muttering that the President has jeopardized the national welfare for the sake of momentary political impact. He withholds dramatic new policies from those who should be consulted for fear the word will leak out and spoil his surprise.

Here are some cases in point:

Surprise No. 1 — Only his closest associates had any advance inkling of his preparations to visit Peking. State Department experts, who are paid by the taxpayers to analyze such moves, weren't consulted. The implications of the trip, therefore, were never "staffed out." The professionals would have urgently advised, for one thing, that the Japanese be consulted. But Prime Minister Sato's government was caught totally by surprise. This undermined Japanese confidence in the U.S. so severely that Japan has made cautious moves to withdraw from the U.S. partnership and go its own way in Asia.

Surprise No. 2 — The President announced his economic about-face without consulting some of his own economic advisers who were still marching in the other direction. But the effect on the Western world of our pulling the dollar out from under it, without advance warning, was wrenching. Two of our staunchest friends, Canada and Japan, publicly threatened retaliation. After the Peking surprise, the economic announcement was a double blow to the Sato government. And our allies in Europe began to re-examine their relations with Moscow, with less regard for the American alliance.

Surprise No. 3 — President Nixon ordered American troops into Cambodia without taking congressional leaders into his confidence. Since wars are supposed to be declared by Congress, his complete failure to consult the legislative branch has created a crisis in the congressional-White House relationship. The resulting distrust has jeopardized the President's legislative programs.

Not only government officials but the public at large has become unsettled by the President's penchant for government-by-surprise. He has presented new policies so often, each with the flourish of a Hollywood extravaganza, that the public is getting jaded. He has kept coming up with new programs, each more dramatic than the past: a New Federalism, a New American Revolution, a New Economics, a New Prosperity. Yet little seems to change, and the new policies seem more fluff than substance. The public is beginning to suspect, therefore, that what Nixon really seeks is a New Campaign Slogan.

Editors, reporters and broadcast journalists are kept off balance through the use of a mixed bag of threats and compliments. When they veer too far from the administration line, Vice President Spiro Agnew is wheeled out for a frontal assault. He cries out for "fair" coverage. What he really means is "favorable" coverage.

For the public's benefit, President Nixon pretends to be unconcerned about his image, deprecating the "experts" who would plaster his beard with makeup or adjust the television lights to hide the bags under his eyes. But this seeming indifference is really part of a studied effort to make his image appear genuine. Actually, the White House is crawling with professional image makers who hide behind a variety of titles but who contribute to presenting the President to the public in the best possible light. Confidential sources put the number at about 55, counting secretaries.

The pattern established for the 1968 campaign became more sophisticated during his first four years in office, and it was this powerful selling machine that he rides into the battle for reelection. He keeps himself surrounded by a team of advertising specialists. But now the entire operation is guided from the top. Nixon dictates the sales policy and hands out the assignments.

As evidence that he had learned the lesson of his disasterous 1960 campaign, he has begun paying attention to how he looks. He fired his barber in October, 1970, and hired Milton Pitts, a tonsorial artist who billed himself as "Washington's leading men's hair stylists." Pitts promptly washed the oil and goo out of Nixon's hair, combed out the curly ends, lowered his sideburns, and gave him a razor cut. Result: A more modern "natural" look. According to one insider, the President was even coloring his hair to hide the gray.

Nixon's tailor, H. Freeman & Son of Philadelphia, began sending the President modestly designed double-breasted suits with wider lapels. Nixon also has started wearing more modern, three-inch-wide neckties. He watches his weight, gets plenty of sleep (seven hours minimum), and shaves as often as three times a day.

The President's image makers, on the other hand, are a somber lot, attired in blue corporate suits, maddeningly efficient, so similar that senators have trouble telling one from the other. But they are professionals. Many are former advertising executives, newsmen, or public relations experts; many worked with Nixon during the 1968 campaign. Of these, most important to the presidential image are his press aides. Whenever Nixon travels, his press staff precedes him, ostensibly to make preparations. Their primary job, however, is to protect the President's image. Before a Nixon visit to Chicago, for example, the aides flew out ahead of him to prepare the press for the great occasion. At one briefing, aide Tim Elbourne outlined for photographers the do's and don't's — mostly don't's.

"What can we do, then?" growled a veteran photographer.

"Well, all of you who want can go with Mrs. Nixon to Goose Lake Prairie," replied Elbroune helpfully. "And we have planned a nice picture of Mr. and Mrs. Nixon stepping off an elevator."

In keeping with the old campaign dictum regarding the press — "keep them comfortable but keep them ignorant" — Nixon had a new press room installed in the White House. Reporters could relax on comfortable suede sofas, walk on thick carpets, and broadcast from spacious booths. There is also a new snack bar. The coffee pots are always kept hot and full, even if the information specialists aren't. Then, having succeeded in keeping the press comfortable, President Nixon has developed a two-fold procedure for evading them. He goes directly to the people by means of television, and he conducts direct mail campaigns. This latter role is performed by none other than helpful Herb Klein, the President's "Director of Information."

The technique is simply to bypass the press in Washington when the administration has a program to sell. Instead, Klein works up a "fact kit" on a particular program and mails it out to the hinterlands to small town editors — many of whom have never before used a source of national news other than the wire services — and they are invariably flattered to get mail directly from the White House. One such mailing, in mid-1971, was a controversial Joseph Alsop column which defended the thrust into Laos and contended that Sen. J. William Fulbright and others "are downright eager to be proved right by an American defeat" in Vietnam.

PARTY SUPPORT

The Republican National Committee, of course, does a prodigious amount of President selling on its own. The party pumps out press releases, magazines and reprints to thousands of editors and publishers in an unending flow. Overseeing this operation is Lyn Nofziger, an affable, portly, hard-nosed politician whose motto is "Don't get mad, get even." Until he moved over to the GOP committee in February, 1971, to become its communications czar, Nofziger was a deputy assistant to the President. He admitted at the time to a "working relationship" with Klein's office. "They know policy and I *have* to know policy, so I'm in contact with them frequently," he said. Speaking for the party, he added, "When you've got a President in the White House, you have to assume the National Committee is an extension. The Democrats sure did."

But for all the image making going on inside the White House, the Nixons never seem quite able to pull off the "First Family" kind of quasi-royalty that Jack and Jackie Kennedy stamped on the presidency. The Nixons would like to recapture the Camelot aura of a decade ago, but as a touch of King Arthur, they always manage to look, somehow, like squares at the Round Table. When President Kennedy outfitted the Marine band in brilliant red coats, people oohed and aahed. But when President Nixon dressed up his White House police in gaudy, Gilbert-and-Sullivan uniforms, people snickered.

The Kennedys introduced theater in the royal tradition to the White House. Their dinners were *de rigueur,* their soirees sparkling. The Nixons have also tried to provide the pageantry of the royal courts at their formal parties. But their interpretation of Camelot is more like a high school production of "The Student Prince." Just as a king of old used to enter his throne room, President Nixon's entry into the East Room for the state dinner is heralded by the blast of trumpets. The Marine buglers, with banners draped from their elongated trumpets, play a fanfare. At this signal, the President descends the grand staircase, with the First Lady on his arm, while the Marine band plays him down with processional music. Nixon takes deliberate, measured steps, beaming benevolently in the manner of monarchs. He is a bit stiff and awkward, however, not having had as much practice as most monarchs. As he enters the East

Room, the band snaps into "Ruffles and Flourishes," followed by the traditional "Hail to the Chief." The music, good but earsplittingly loud, fills the room. Later, when the Nixons pass from the East Room into the State dining room, crewcut military aides bedecked with medals and braids stand starchily at attention in two rows.

Dinner guests are surrounded all evening by an impressive swirl of military uniforms. In addition to the dashing military aides, as many as half a dozen military musical units might be pressed into service to serenade the guests. Jacqueline Kennedy started the tradition of continuous music, and the Nixons continued the tradition, granting no more than a few seconds between numbers, until the last guest leaves.

When President Nixon entertained the astronauts in Los Angeles in 1969, the musicians alone filled two huge Air Force transport planes. "Sometimes," one of the musicians told newsmen, "I feel as if I am fiddling while Rome burns." He referred to the Pomp and Circumstance inside the White House, as contrasted with the trouble and turmoil outside. Agreed another White House intimate: "The white-gloved Negro waiters, the garishly uniformed military aides, the red-coated orchestra in the foyer, all give a feeling of isolation from NOW."

For the Nixons, entertaining seems to be more a duty than a pleasure. Said an insider: "I have never seen the President rub elbows or mingle with his guests in an informal way. He will either sit down at a dinner table or stand in a reception line. When he gave a reception for UN diplomats at the Waldorf in New York City, he took up his position in the reception line as soon as he arrived. He shook hands for two hours until all the guests had passed. Then he left."

At the White House, too, the Nixons often retire early while their guests are still milling around. Nixon has done away with most of the traditional White House receptions. He prefers formal dinners. "I think I know the reason," said one aide. "The President loves to make after-dinner speeches." The speeches are mostly of the Rotarian, mutual-admiration variety.

Despite all the trumpets and the fanfare, most White House guests probably would agree that Richard Nixon's Camelot is still more Middle America than Middle England.

"...WE PRECIOUS FEW..."

At a White House party some years ago, a sedate businessman lost control of his emotions. He turned suddenly red around the eyes, and tears washed down his cheeks.

"What's the matter?" asked President Eisenhower in alarm.

"I just wanted to tell you, Mr. President," sobbed the businessman, "what it has meant to me to spend an evening at the White House."

His feelings will be understood only by the favored few who have been ushered by glittering military aides down the red-carpeted corridor to a White House social function. The most coveted invitation in America today is the gold-crested, hand-lettered form which declares: "The President and Mrs. Richard M. Nixon request the pleasure of your company." No matter who may be in residence, a White House invitation is the closest thing in the country to a command appearance.

The idea that the President would play politics with the White House guest list is not entirely beyond suspicion. Few people are so blase, as all Presidents well know, that they would not cherish an evening at the White House. Not only Nixon but his predecessors have used White House invitations to reward campaign contributors, political allies, helpful Congressmen and friendly newsmen.

Almost everyone who has the President's ear is eager to suggest who should be invited to White House soirees. For a state dinner, the protocol office always submits a proposed guest list. A powerful Congressman may request that a favorite constituent be invited. A political fund raiser may remind the President of some deserving contributor. Often the Vice President, Cabinet officers and White House aides will have names to suggest.

The names are forwarded to the social secretary who draws up a tentative guest list. This is submitted to the First Lady, who checks over the guests to make sure they're acceptable and compatible. Usually she makes a few substitutions of her own. (Lady Bird Johnson, for instance, was partial to people who helped with her beautification projects.) But the President is the final social arbiter.

In Washington's politically sensitive society, where status is as fragile as a crystal champagne glass, the White House guest list is the unofficial social index. It also provides a valuable insight for lobbyists, diplomats, society reporters and other Washington watchers as to who's "in" at the White House. During the LBJ years, for instance, Arthur Krim, president of United Artists, was in; Don Kendall, president of Pepsi-Cola, was out. Actor Kirk Douglas was in; John Wayne was out. Mrs. Rebecca Harkness, wealthy New York widow, was in; Mrs. Helen Clay Frick, millionaire Pittsburgh widow, was out. Comedian Jimmie Durante was in; Jackie Gleason was out.

Generally speaking, the Johnsons placed more emphasis on conviviality than protocol. They would invite such disparate guests as actor Gene Kelly and photographer Edward Steichen and seat them across from one another, not without lively success.

The Johnsons were the first to give a cookout at the White House, a savory affair with the President supervising the charcoal grills. Unlike President Eisenhower, who had a bum knee, and President Kennedy, who had a bad back, LBJ loved to dance through the night. Sometimes, he would keep doing it until every lady at the party could boast next day that she had danced with the President. Other times, he would latch onto a favorite and monopolize her most of the evening. Once he grabbed singer Roberta Peters, danced with her until midnight, then escorted her on a private midnight tour of the White House.

President Nixon has restored more dignity and protocol to White House affairs. His wife, Pat, read *Washington Post* reporter Marie Smith's book, *Entertaining in the White House*, for tips on how past First Ladies handled parties, and then followed suit.

The President, being what he is, must draw the line on his guest list in some instances; he cannot be as liberal as he might personally choose to be. Indonesia's former President Sukarno, for example, tried to bring his girl friend instead of his wife to a state dinner in his honor. The State Department explained tactfully that space limitations would prohibit anyone under the rank of Cabinet from attending. Sukarno thereupon swore in the lady as a minister and brought her anyway.

When a chief of state from Latin America imbibed too freely of White House liqueurs, President Kennedy recognized the signs and discreetly escorted his distinguished guest to the library on the pretext of presenting him with a copy of his book, *Profiles of Courage*. In the middle of the presentation, the potentate lapsed into a drunken sleep, and another international "crisis" was averted.

President Nixon is using the White House to throw fund-raising dinners for the Republican campaign chest. He invites fat cats to the White House for quiet, *de rigueur* dinners. Afterward, over Sancerre and cigars, they are hit up for political contributions. Few financial tycoons can resist an invitation to dine at the White House, and they arrive resplendent in black tie and tux to be plucked. To preserve the presidential dignity, Nixon doesn't stay around for the sordid financial pitch. He makes some lofty remarks about peace and prosperity, then discreetly departs before the money tree is shaken.

The latest White House fund raiser was held on April 8 less than three weeks after the President declared on TV his firm support for limiting campaign contributions. A glittering gathering of Illinois millionaires, dressed in their fancy duds, munched on delectables from the White House kitchen and listened to the President talk. He told how he was turning the Vietnam war over to the Vietnamese and said he was sorry he hadn't followed his own advice when he urged stock market speculators to start buying a year ago. He started to leave, paused to listen respectfully to Illinois Gov. Richard Ogilvie, then made good his escape.

Thereupon, lesser White House celebrities took over and began to warm up the group for the plucking. Even Harry Dent, the President's

Southern strategist, joined in the political evangelism. "Southerners just love the President," oozed Dent in his best Dixie dialect. First on his feet to offer financial aid was insurance tycoon W. Clement Stone, perhaps the sweetest sugar daddy of them all, who contributed a traceable $650,000 to the GOP in 1968, another $1 million in 1970 through a maze of channels. But the willing Stone, who resembles the late comedian Robert Benchley, has received unfavorable publicity for his beneficence. Presumably with this in mind, R. Douglas Stuart, the Quaker Oats magnate, suggested bluntly that Clem Stone's name ought to be kept out of their fund-raising effort. "You are absolutely right," said Stone amiably. "I agree with you completely."

In the awesome atmosphere of the White House, full of good food and drink, the money men offered little resistance. Indeed, the fat cats are expected to line up for a chance to be dunned at a White House dinner. And the rustle of every unfolding bill and the scratch of pen on check add emphasis to the need for reforming the greatest evil in the American political system.

The President pays out of his own pocket for those parties that are strictly private, but the bills for other White House entertainment is picked up by the taxpayer. How much they pay for the President's good time is carefully concealed. He draws an entertainment and travel allowance of $40,000 a year. But he can always dip into another $50,000 expense allowance to pay for parties. In addition, he can charge his diplomatic entertainment, if he wishes, to the State Department. The money is siphoned from a million-dollar fund that is appropriated each year for "emergencies in the diplomatic and consular service.' No government auditor has been bold enough to check the various accounts to see how much the President spends on entertainment.

How can one get an invitation to a White House party? Only with great difficulty — unless, of course, you are a big campaign contributor, or have great political influence. Otherwise the chances are strong you'll just have to read about them in the newspaper.

"THAT LITTLE OL' WINEMAKER. . ."

To the dismay of American winemakers, President Nixon serves French and German wines almost exclusively at White House soirees. This violates the drinking decrees of his own Administration which, in the cause of patriotism of the palate, encourages officials to ply their guests with American wines.

The State Department, for its part, has issued a stern memo on the subject. Diplomats who throw parties for their country are instructed to serve American wines "to reduce the balance of payments problem as well as to stimulate market interest in American wines abroad." The wine orders for President Nixon's *de rigueur* affairs, however, are prepared in woeful disregard for the balance of payments. He traitorously offers German Schloss Johannisberg and French Chateau Margaux to visiting dignitaries. John F. Kennedy, who was fond enough of wines, and Lyndon B. Johnson, who preferred Scotch to Sancerre, always served American wines at the White House.

The change in the White House wine list is particularly galling to the Republicans who represent America's wine country in Congress. Not only does their own President favor foreign wines, but he is a native of California where most of the grape vines grow.

Don Clausen, the Congressman from California's Napa Valley, who demonstrates his own loyalty by keeping bottles of American Cabernet Sauvignon and Chenin Blanc in his congressional liquor cabinet in place of the usual whiskey, registered a vigorous dissent over Nixon's wine policies. Clausen is a loyal Republican who has backed the President on everything from Saigon to the SST. The least the President could do in return, Clausen feels, is drink Napa Valley wine.

In a private letter to the President, Clausen appealed, "The issue at stake, Mr. President, is not so much one of excluding foreign wines, rather a desire to put America first in this field. We would hope that, where possible, a minimum ratio of two American to one foreign wine serving be the policy unless, of course, there are some unusual or extenuating diplomatic circumstances." He conceded, for instance, that it would be "appropriate to serve French wines" to France's President Pompidou or to offer German wines to "high officials from Germany." But to serve foreign wines to dignitaries from wineless countries, he felt, was absolutely abhorrent. Rep. James Hasting, another Nixon loyalist who represents the wineries of upstate New York, has also split with the President over his taste in wines.

One White House insider, alluding to the President's after-dinner drinking habits, confided, "I don't think he knows the difference between a good American and French claret. He's just got some snooty advisors."

RANK HAS ITS PRIVILEGE

Besides a $90,000 total entertainment fund available to the President, Nixon was given a pay raise his first year in office from $100,000 to $200,000. His fringe benefits, which cover everything from floral arrangements to free medical care, are also the most generous on earth. The taxpayers even paid for a special shark net to keep predatory fish from nipping at Mr. Nixon when he goes swimming at Key Biscayne, Florida.

But surely the most extravagant gesture of the Nixon Administration is the royal treatment ordered for King Timahoe in his travels across this country. King Timahoe is Nixon's handsome Irish setter, and he was flown cross-country in a luxury class Air Force jet. The gesture evaporated those threadbare days in 1952 when Nixon cried to the voters about his little mongrel Checkers and his wife's cloth coat. It was in the summer of 1970 we caught the White House dispatching the presidential mutt from Washington, D.C. to San Clemente, California, in a remodeled 707 with the same pampering usually accorded high officials.

Of course, this elevation of pets has been a ruler's prerogative since the Emperor Caligula gave his horse, Incitatus, a retinue of slaves and announced the horse would be made a consul. Nixon, in this tradition, summoned King Timahoe to San Clemente that summer. At Andrews Air Force Base, outside Washington, officers were wryly informed only that an "important personage" would accompany White House aides to California. To their astonishment, the "important personage" turned out to be the dog, tongue lolling, coat sleek as a four-star general's. One anti-canine member of the traveling party said King Timahoe was treated more like a dignitary than a dog. At San Clemente, when the dog first disembarked, observers at the airport thought the trip had been made by King Timahoe in regal solitude. But the setter, named after the hometown of Nixon's Irish Milhous forebears, had merely left the plane separately. The presidential dog's travels across country since 1970 have been kept top-secret. But invariably, he appears in San Clemente when his distinguished master is there.

The White House has never limited the space on presidential planes to dogs. In June that year when the President sent a group of governors, senators and congressmen to Indochina to study the war, they airlifted back some artificial animals. At Saigon, the distinguished passengers became entranced by some glazed ceramic elephants. Republican and Democratic bigwigs alike sent out government underlings to buy them up as status gifts for GOP friends. By the time the plane was ready to go, the delegates had acquired 45 of the large ceramic pachyderms. Enroute back to Washington, the elephant buyers decided it would be politically disastrous for news photographers to catch them deplaning from a "war mission" laden with expensive, silly-looking elephants. The Customs Bureau had already agreed to clear them with whatever gifts they brought in, so the stage was set for the great elephant smuggle. The sumptuous Air Force airliner taxied in. Newsmen and cameramen rushed up. Somber as only all-night partyers and brainwashed briefees can be, the delegates told of the ordeals they had gone through. Only after the newsmen had left were the glazed elephants quietly unloaded and delivered to the delegation members. Footnote: The VIP traffic at Andrews Air Force Base picks up around Christmas time. In December, 1970, no less than four "classified" plane loads of junketeering congressmen and officials arrived at the base with Santa-loads of gifts for themselves and friends. These included furniture, lamps, vases, $1,000 antiques, all hauled through Andrews gates while custom agents looked the other way. Ordinary citizens can bring in only $100 worth of duty-free gifts.

PRESIDENTIAL SECURITY

The assassination of President Kennedy in 1963 and the bombing of the Capitol building in 1971 raised urgent questions about White House security. Could a bomb be planted anywhere near the President today? Could another President be shot down? The reassuring opinion is that, while it's still possible, it would be much more difficult. The White House now sits in the center of an electronic entanglement to detect intruders that seems infallible.

Back in Lyndon Johnson's days, the Secret Service ran a security test at Camp David and succeeded in infiltrating the presidential retreat in Maryland's Catoctin Mountains. The Marines who guard Camp David sheepishly tightened their security. But similar attempts to penetrate the White House grounds have failed. Infiltration teams have never been able to slip past the all-seeing electronic eyes that the Secret Service began installing around the White House in the early 50's.

In 1961, someone managed to flip a hand grenade — happily, a dud — over the fence. It went undetected until a member of the ground crew ran over it with a lawn mower. But even this harmless, unpublicized incident probably couldn't go unnoticed today. The tourists who stream through the White House five days a week are hustled through the historic rooms and are kept under constant surveillance.

As for assassination attempts on the President when he is traveling or making public appearances, "The Secret Service is confident that, had its new intelligence system been in effect in 1963, the activities of Lee Harvey Oswald would have brought him to the attention of the Secret Service before the fatal attack on President Kennedy." This statement is lifted from the 1969 report by the National Commission on the Causes and Prevention of Violence, headed by Milton Eisenhower.

In support of the report, it should be noted that the Secret Service, whose duty is to protect the President at all times, has more than three times as many agents today (1,021) as it had when John Kennedy took office in 1961. Director James J. Rowley has intensified the training of agents and has put together an intelligence system that now includes a computerized list of extremists and crackpots who, for whatever reason, have been singled out for special attention. But actually, the Secret Service is more worried about the distinguished visitors, newsmen, aides and even bodyguards who have personal access to the President. Distinguished visitors can't be searched without offending them, and the most trusted associates can go berserk.

It happened during the Eisenhower era; the mind of a White House correspondent suddenly snapped during a presidential trip. He was one of the trusted White House regulars, representing a great New York newspaper. He was overheard by the late Merriman Smith, famed White House reporter for UPI, muttering incoherently that he intended to kill the President. Smith lunged at the man and grabbed him around the neck. There was a brief tussle. The New York reporter slammed Smith to the floor and stomped on his face before the Secret Service agents moved in and hustled the berserk correspondent away.

Security is necessarily intensive around Air Force One, the presidential plane. All luggage is carefully inspected for hidden weapons or bombs. Crewmen are ordered never to let the baggage out of their sight. On rare occasions, a crewman has turned away from the luggage long enough to buy cigarettes or a Coke. It's usually then that Air Force security men quickly, quietly take advantage of the lapse to plant a smoke bomb in the luggage. When the crewman discovers the smoking luggage in flight, he is harshly reminded that it could have been a real bomb.

CIA ASSASSINATIONS?

Assassination always raises questions and fears, President Kennedy's no more than the plot to kill Cuban dictator Fidel Castro, hidden for 10 years from the public. The Castro plot raises ugly questions that officials would just as soon keep buried inside the Central Intelligence Agency.

1. Has the CIA tried to assassinate any other leaders? John McCone, who headed the CIA during the six attempts to knock off Castro, denied emphatically that the CIA has tried to kill anyone. But former Senator George Smathers, one of John F. Kennedy's closest friends, told us that the late President suspected that the CIA had arranged the shootings of the Dominican Republic's Rafael Trujillo in 1961 and South Vietnam's Ngo Dinh Diem in 1963.

2. Did President Kennedy personally sanction the plot against Castro? The preparations to assassinate the Cuban dictator began during the last

months of the Eisenhower administration as part of the Bay of Pigs scheme. All six attempts, however, were made during 1961-63 when Kennedy occupied the White House. Smathers told us he once spoke to the late President about assassinating Castro. Kennedy merely rolled back his eyes, recalled Smathers, as if to indicate the idea was too wild to discuss. Subsequently, Kennedy told Smathers of his suspicion that the CIA may have been behind the Trujillo and Diem assassinations.

3. Did the late Robert Kennedy know about the assassination attempts? After the Bay of Pigs fiasco, President Kennedy swore to friends he would like "to splinter the CIA in a thousand pieces and scatter it to the winds." He put his brother, Robert, in charge of the CIA with instructions to shake it up. The CIA made five attempts on Castro's life after the Bay of Pigs while Robert Kennedy was riding herd on the agency.

4. Could the plot against Castro have backfired against President Kennedy? The late President was murdered nine months after the last assassination team was caught on a Havana rooftop with high-powered rifles. Presumably, they were subjected to fiendish tortures until they told all they knew. None of the assassination teams, however, had direct knowledge of the CIA involvement. The CIA instigators had represented themselves as oilmen seeking revenge against Castro for his seizure of oil holdings.

A BROTHER'S ANGUISH

Former associates recall that Robert Kennedy, deeply despondent, went into semi-seclusion after his brother's assassination. Could he have been tormented by more than natural grief? He certainly learned that the assassin, Lee Harvey Oswald, had been active in the pro-Castro movement and had traveled to Mexico to visit the Cuban Embassy a few weeks before the dreadful day in Dallas. Could Bob Kennedy have been plagued by the terrible thought that the CIA plot, which he must at least have condoned, put into motion forces that may have brought about his brother's martyrdom? The last surviving brother, Senator Edward Kennedy (D-Mass.), gives no insight. His brothers had never spoken to him about any assassination attempts against Castro, he says. But he claims he was aware that Senator Smathers had talked to the late President about eliminating Castro.

Smathers told us that President Kennedy seemed "horrified" at the idea of political assassinations. "I remember him saying," recalled Smathers, "that the CIA frequently did things he didn't know about, and he was unhappy about it. He complained that the CIA was almost autonomous. He told me he believed the CIA had arranged to have Diem and Trujillo bumped off. He was pretty well shocked about that. He thought it was a stupid thing to do, and he wanted to get control of what the CIA was doing."

McCone disagrees vigorously with Smathers. He has insisted that "no plot was authorized or implemented" to assassinate Castro, Trujillo, Diem or anyone else. "During those days of tension, there was a wide spectrum of plans ranging from one extreme to another," McCone has admitted. "Whenever this subject (assassinating Castro) was brought up — and it was — it was rejected immediately on two grounds. First, it would not be condoned by anybody, Second, it wouldn't have achieved anything."

There was also talk in high places, McCone acknowledges, of supporting a coup to oust Diem. The former CIA director said he had argued against this at a secret session with both Kennedy brothers. He had contended that there was no one strong enough to take Diem's place and that a coup, therefore, would bring "political upheaval."

"I told the President and Bobby together," recalled McCone, "that if I were running a baseball team and had only one pitcher, I wouldn't take him out of the game."

The November, 1963, coup caught the U.S. completely by surprise, he said. While the plotters were moving on the palace, he said, Ambassador Henry Cabot Lodge was visiting Diem. Admiral Ulysess Sharp, then our Pacific commander, had also been present, but left early to go to the airport. McCone said President Diem escaped through a tunnel but was caught in nearby Cholon and "shot in a station wagon."

CHANGING OF THE GUARD

One of the aspects of American politics that most intrigues and baffles foreign observers is how the national government manages to change hands with such comparative ease every four years or so. Like a magic act, they see it but they can't believe it. But it's a fact that the country's business is carried on right through the periods of transition. There are rendings and abrasions, of course, but all in all the amputation of one party and the grafting of another are done with a minimum of trauma. Here's how the Republicans managed it in 1969.

The Johnson Administration prepared briefing books on every facet of government for the Nixon Administration. But like the men who accompany every new President, Nixon's men had their own ideas. The Inaugural Committee, meanwhile, found bipartisan support for one of the most pressing problems of the day. It paid $70,000 to have the big trees along the route from the White House to the Capitol sprayed with a substance to chase away starlings and protect the new President from an old Washington hazard.

In preparation for the takeover, Nixon had announced he would seek the best minds in the nation to help him govern. As he phrased it, his would be a "government drawn from the broadest possible base, an Administration made up of Republicans, Democrats and independents." It would include, he promised, "the very best men and women I can find in the country — from business, from government, from labor, from all the areas." As it happened, oddly enough, "the very best men and women... in the country" were all male, all white, all Christian and all Republican. There apparently was not a woman, not a black, nor a Jew in the nation worthy of serving in the Nixon cabinet. Not until 1971 did a Democrat, whose views were largely indistinguishable from Nixon's, finally make it.

When Nixon looked around for an attorney general, he went directly to the source that had given him leaders in every phase of his 1968 election campaign — his own law firm. And naturally he tagged John Mitchell for the job because Mitchell had brought in more business, more profit than any other member of their Wall Street firm. To Nixon, this was qualification enough. No matter that Mitchell's law experience was virtually limited to the bond business; he was the man to head up the new administration's Justice Department.

The William Rogers-Richard Nixon combination dated back to the Alger Hiss days in 1948 and continued through the slush fund scandal of 1952. Rogers was always the mentor, Nixon the eager student. Rogers, although he had been attorney general under Eisenhower, suffered from a dearth of background in foreign affairs — precisely the quality Nixon was looking for in his Secretary of State. But then, Rogers has been quoted as saying there was no foreign policy problem that he couldn't learn to cope with after three hours study.

Then there was Nixon's political crony from California, Robert Finch. For reasons never fully explained he wanted more than anything to try his hand at that model of bureaucratic insanity, the Department of Health, Education and Welfare. The most unmanageable among all Washington departments, HEW stood as whimsical challenge to Finch and finally crushed him. Later both he and Nixon recognized the error of their decisions and Finch bowed out as gracefully as the news media would permit.

The President did attempt to recruit some Democrats, though. He turned to the Vietnam Hawk, Senator Henry Jackson of Washington, to head the Defense Department, but Jackson declined and the post went to Melvin Laird. The impotent post of Ambassador to the United Nations was offered in turn to Hubert Humphrey, Sargent Shriver and Eugene

McCarthy, all top names on the Democrat roster. All turned it down. But Nixon did not despair. He finally was able to enroll a token Democrat to his team. Daniel Patrick Moynihan, whose ghetto essays had most black leaders frothing at the mouth, would preside over the administration's Council on Urban Affairs, and one day suggest in a memo that government continue a policy of "benign neglect" toward the Negro.

Aside from Moynihan, the Administration was Republican, through and through. Nixon and his entourage were all of a kind: unhumorous, dark-suited, white-shirted, clean-shaven and square. Although Nixon tried hard to entertain with the elegance of the Kennedys and the gusto of the Johnsons, his parties still came out like a chaperoned tea dance for teenagers.

Periodically, a new device is tried out in Washington to shoo starlings from the eaves of government buildings. The startled birds rise fluttering and twittering, then settle back again when the threat has subsided. It's the same way with government bureaucrats: a new administration moves in, shouts about changes, may even make a few, moves some furniture, issues solemn warnings and then gets about the business of running the government. And the bureaucrats, like the starlings, flutter and twitter for a week or so, and then settle back to their old roosts.

BUREAUCRACY

Many years ago bureaucracy meant simply the administration of a government chiefly through bureaus; today, millions of tons of triplicates later, bureaucracy is the snide tag for a government, any government, marked by diffusion of authority among numerous offices and an adamant adherence to inflexible rules of operation.

First to pinpoint this decline (or rise, depending on the viewpoint) of the bureaucracy was C. Northcote Parkinson in his internationally famous "Parkinson's Law" theorems which he published and expanded at various times. A few random observations expressed by Parkinson have become world-wide maxims:

Work expands so as to fill the time available for its completion.

Subordinates multiply at a fixed rate, regardless of the amount of work produced.

Expenditure rises to meet income.

When funds are limited, the only economy made is in thinking.

All that we buy with higher taxes is additional administrative delay.

Satirical as these theorems appear, there is ample documentation testifying that Parkinson's Law is not 100 per cent put-on. On the contrary, there are great lumps of universal truth floating in it, as a quick glance at the U.S. presidency will prove.

THE PRESIDENT

Like every President before him, Richard Nixon has issued directives, delivered pronouncements, dictated memos and otherwise sought to bestir the vast federal bureaucracy. He has put on a personal show of efficiency and has sounded solemn warnings that he expects renewed vigor from all federal workers. But also like every past President, Nixon has made little impression upon the bureaucrats who respectfully note the presidential stirrings and then go on doing as they have always done.

Thoroughly frustrated, he fusses over the negative attitudes of most bureaucrats, fumes at their can't-be-done responses to his new ideas and chafes over the bureaucratic inertia he encounters. In exasperation, he has complained that government officials "spend one-half of their time writing papers to each other." He cites, as an illustration, the excess paper work that Washington demands from local and state authorities in return for federal grants. Over 30 major steps, involving more than 100 different forms and reports, often are required for a simple $1,000 grant.

Nixon's predecessors must be smiling indulgently on high. Franklin D. Roosevelt after struggling with the Naval bureaucracy compared the encounter to "boxing a featherbed." Dwight D. Eisenhower, who masterminded history's largest war, wound up on the losing side in what he called "the battle of Washington." And John F. Kennedy wryly likened his experience with the bureaucracy to "grappling with a whale." Then came Richard Nixon to grapple with the whale. After a year or two of valiant struggle, he found himself in the whale's belly looking out.

The bureaucratic phenomenon is wondrous to observe. Like a giant amoeba, it sort of slurps along, a shapeless blob, following the path of least resistance. It pushes out in every direction, and its substance flows into the bulges. When it encounters a morsel, the bureaucratic amoeba flows around it and absorbs it. And when the bureaucracy can no longer contain its own bulk, it simply divides — one into two, two into four, and so on. Today one amoeba, tomorrow 16.

From another view, the federal apparatus resembles a marvelous, monstrous factory, which is engaged in the manufacture of a single, basic product: Confusion. Call it the Fuddle Factory. The maze of bureaucratic wheels, cogs and gears, spinning in different directions, often countering each other, would delight a Rube Goldberg. All the whirling and whirring creates the illusion of great industry. For all its movement, however, the Fuddle Factory goes nowhere.

The actual dimensions of the bureaucracy are known to no man, but some inklings can be gained from the 1967 Census of Governments. These figures show that an astounding 81,299 government entities now exist in the United States. The breakdown:

U.S. government	1
State governments	50
Local governments	81,248
Counties	3,049
Municipalities	18,048
Townships	17,105
School districts	21,782
Special districts	21,264
Grand Total	81,299

All this lays to eternal rest the notion that a missile is the most complex contrivance known to man, for each of the 81,299 entities of government is a moving part. Within each entity are other moving parts, wheels within wheels, all going round and round.

Consider the U.S. government. George Washington started out with nine executive agencies, employing a grand total of 1,000 federal workers. From this small bureaucratic beginning, the federal government has spread and swollen into a crazy patchwork of nearly 2,000 agencies, each itself a conglomeration of bureaus, sections, divisions and committees.

Out of sheer desperation, President Nixon has threatened "massive personnel cuts in every area of government." This betrays a certain naivete, however, about the bureaucracy's powers of self-preservation.

The Fuddle Factory constantly finds more, not less, fuddling to do. Lacking constructive work, the Fuddle Factory turns inward and produces for itself rather than for the people it is supposed to serve. Hence the bureaucratic dictum: expand or expire.

The Bureau of Indian Affairs provides an example. In 1970, on the Pine Ridge Reservation in western South Dakota, the Oglala Sioux are recipients of $8,040 per household in bureaucratic services. About 1,400 government officials work full-time on the reservation, and an additional 425 work part-time. This doesn't include additional hundreds who work in district, area and regional offices. The Fuddle Factory, then, could provide a live-in bureaucrat for every Oglala family. Thus has fuddling become a fine art — from the most remote reservation to the fuddle capital of the free world in Washington.

THE BUREAUCRATS

Certain symbols are held sacred by the bureaucrat, who, as evidence perhaps that hot air rises, often ascends to high office in the land. How high his standing is determined in exacting detail by such ornaments as his office acreage, rug plushness, furniture array, and limousine service. He is known, too, by his dining, parking, washroom, and elevator privileges. Whether he sips water from a silver decanter, brown plastic jug, or water fountain in the corridor is another sign of his status. The protocol extends even to dog licenses, the lower numbers going to the pooches of the more prominent.

A bureaucrat's immediate domain, his office, provides the real clues to his importance. Is it large enough, say, for football scrimmage? Is there a trim of woodwork around the walls? What color is the rug and how deep is its pile? Is the desk kingsize? Is there a flag stand? A sofa suitable for taking naps? These are the trivia from which the measure of the man is taken.

For sheer size and splendor, few grand ballrooms can compare with a cabinet member's office. The Secretary of State's sumptuous suite, for instance, not only could accommodate a United Nations session, it could provide the delegates with built-in television, meals from an electric range, and washroom and shower facilities.

In the Pentagon, status works outward from the interior "A" ring of the five-sided colossus. An individual's advancement is measured by his progress toward the outer "E" ring which the top brass inhabit. The civilian chiefs (Assistant Secretaries and above) are entitled to a fresh paint job and new wall-to-wall carpeting when they move in. But the real yardstick is a three-foot trim of woodwork around the walls. Enter a Pentagon office with this executive paneling, and one is dealing with a man of consequence. Also, only the highest ranks ride the Pentagon elevators; all others must use the stairs or escalators.

Who's who in federal bureaucracy can also be calculated by the sleekness of their limousines. The Cadillacs, Lincolns and Chrysler Imperials carry the top brass; the Chevrolets, Fords and Plymouths transport the lesser officials. The line-up of glossy government cars at any big Washington function is enough to take a taxpayer's breath away. Cabinet officers are permitted to use their glory wagons for private as well as business purposes, and their wives often are driven to the supermarket in sumptuous style. This is a sore point with Senators, who have no standing at the government motor pool, and Supreme Court Justices, who have one car among them. Only the Chief Justice and Senate and House leaders are entitled to limousine services.

Next to a limousine, a parking sticker is the most prized badge of distinction. The State Department provides only one parking space for every seven employees. The situation is even worse surrounding other government buildings. The Commerce Department, for instance, has 190 parking spaces for more than 4,100 employees.

The worst sticklers for protocol — as might be expected — are the brass hats. There is a constant stir, for example, over who should be allowed to embellish his hat with scrambled-egg designs. It used to be that no one below Navy captain or Army-Air Force colonel could wear this golden scroll. Then the Navy opened the privilege to commanders, and the Army responded by authorizing scrambled-egg hats for majors. Finally, the status seekers in the Air Force are including lieutenant colonels.

The most coveted symbol of Army status is tenancy in one of the cavernous, barn-like houses along "Brass Row" at Fort Myer, Virginia. Senior Admirals are scattered around town in Navy homes, but they have had their status troubles, too. When Arthur Radford became the first Admiral to head the Joint Chiefs of Staff, there arose the prickliest of protocol problems. The Navy chief traditionally lives in a rambling old house at the Naval Observatory. Admiral and Mrs. Robert Carney were ensconced there. But since Radford outranked Carney, the question arose: could the Carneys be evicted? This became a battle of the wives. Mrs. Carney egged her husband into getting a ruling from the Navy's legal department that the Observatory house was the official residence of the Navy chief. Thus she outmaneuvered Mrs. Radford who threatened to pull her husband's rank but ended up in a three-story, eight-bedroom house formerly occupied by a mere Rear Admiral.

The Pentagon's civilian chiefs, once initiated to the privileges of rank, sometimes become even more protocol-minded than the brass hats. When former Assistant Army Secretary Arthur Sylvester learned that he was entitled to fly a five-star flag on his auto fender, he not only insisted upon displaying the flag but once stopped the car to unfurl it when it became wrapped around its staff.

THEIR VICTIMS

Despite the maxims of Parkinson's Law, the thrashings about of the bureaucracy are not always fatuous. Often, they're downright menacing to the taxpayer. To protect themselves from the dishonest and the disloyal, the American people may have created a Frankenstein's monster which is turning on the citizens it is supposed to serve. This is the relentless and rapacious federal enforcement complex which has produced a new and frightening trend toward government-by-investigation. The federal bureaucracy is literally crawling with investigators who, if they are to earn their salaries, must investigate *someone*. Today, this could be almost anyone who deals with the government or makes out a tax return.

It has become an all too frequent practice, in conflicts between private citizens and federal agencies, for the government to try to settle disputes by investigating the disputants. The power of investigation, which is supposed to be used for the good of the citizens, is often used instead to intimidate, coerce, and strike back at persons who challenge the rulings or oppose the policies of the government.

The contractor who won't accept the government's terms, the taxpayer who contests a ruling, even the associate of someone else under investigation may find himself hounded by gumshoes. Of course, the government has no power to prosecute innocent men. So an ambitious federal agency, seeking to extend its authority, must create new criminals. This is done by passing new laws or reinterpreting the old ones, thus producing guilt where none had previously existed. Then out swarm the investigators, those faceless men in blue serge suits, to look for violators. A top General Services Administration official has admitted, "We used to have a large staff of engineers and a few lawyers and investigators. Now we have a large staff of lawyers and investigators and a few engineers."

The government has spun such a web of regulations, each new agency adding to the tangle, that it is almost impossible for a citizen to go about his business without committing violations. More than 50 permanent agencies, employing 2.8 million people, oversee every phase of life from teaching birth control or baby care to prescribing burial methods. The federal government has make-or-break power over more than 40 per cent of the nation's businesses. The regulatory agencies, for example, can all but destroy any transportation, telephone, electric, or radio-television company simply by giving the thumbscrews an extra twist.

These regulatory agencies, if they are to justify the expansion dear to the hearts of all bureaucrats, must constantly find more people to investigate. Since June 30, 1961, the Securities and Exchange Commission, to select only one, has almost doubled its payroll. Each new employee has brought a corresponding boost in investigative zeal. Comments Barron's, the national financial weekly, "The SEC and its friends are seeking new worlds to conquer. They are questioning the propriety of financial public relations. They are moving in on corporate accounting practices. They are whittling away at management's right to buy and sell."

In theory, an innocent person has nothing to fear from investigators. But once the gumshoes have come around questioning a citizen's neighbors and associates, a cloud of suspicion is raised that may never be dispelled. His reputation may be ruined even though he is innocent of any wrongdoing.

Although most federal officials try to be fair and most agencies do not condone coercive investigations, the bureaucratic system tends to uphold the abuses of those few entrenched office holders who regard themselves as the masters rather than the servants of the people. They usually are able to summon the massive weight of the U.S. government behind their rulings and recommendations, for most agency heads, unfamiliar with the details of a case, are inclined to accept the judgment of their subordinates. Investigators in particular are held sacrosanct in many federal bureaus. Once they start bloodhounding a case, only the boldest bureaucrat would dare intervene. "It isn't safe to stick your nose into an investigation," said one official. "What if the guy turns out to be guilty? The next thing you know, the inspectors will be trying to link *you* to the case."

When the SEC rejected an investigator's recommendation that a Connecticut company be indicted for fraud, the agent bounced back his recommendation in even stronger words. The SEC commissioners, nervous that they might be accused of a whitewash, decided to pass the buck to the Justice Department. The case went to a U.S. attorney who later admitted there was insufficient evidence for an indictment. But he didn't want to take the responsibility for overruling the agency. Playing it safe, he submitted the matter to a grand jury which in turn felt he wouldn't have presented the case if an indictment weren't justified. Result: company officials were duly indicted, though no one except the original investigator thought they deserved to be. The trial jury, of course, found them innocent — after two years of mental anguish, federal harassment, and legal expense.

THE INTERNAL REVENUE SERVICE

A favorite harassment device of the bureaucracy is to toss difficult cases, no matter how unrelated they may be to taxes, to the Internal Revenue Service. "A lot of agencies like to use us," former Commissioner Sheldon Cohen once acknowledged. "We try to discourage this, but these disputes often have tax overtones."

The IRS would like its agents to be loved. To this end, it tries eagerly to make more friendly contact with the public. Originally called the Internal Revenue Bureau, it dropped the "Bureau" for "Service" because the agency chiefs felt the former word had too harsh a ring. They wanted to emphasize that their job was to help the taxpayer, not merely pluck him. The 6,000 collectors have been designated "revenue officers" to get away from the old stigma of their calling. The word "warrant" has been deleted from final tax notices because of its unduly frightening connotation. A special committee has examined all form letters to make sure they contain no implied threats or disagreeable language.

But, as in any large organization, petty tyrants do exist. Even an occasional misfit turns up. A Washington attorney was given such a rough time over his taxes that he started checking on the agent's background. It turned out that the revenue man was an escapee from Baltimore's Shepherd Pratt insane asylum. A paranoid type, he believed himself to be the illegitimate son of the late President Woodrow Wilson and the Duchess of Kent. This is, of course, a unique case. The great majority of Internal Revenue employees are decent, hard-working people doing their best in a difficult, unpopular job to serve both the government and the public. Yet hardships and inequalities, perhaps inevitable when a great bureaucratic machine begins to grind, do exist. Tax disputes, more than any other problems, have given many harassed citizens a glimpse of the face of Uncle Sam when he scowls.

When the government moved to take over private housing on military bases, owners who resisted were suddenly besieged by tax agents. The Justice Department's Land Acquisition Section brought tax pressure, for example, to bear on Nashville builder Edward Carmack, who was unwilling to sell 600 homes at Stewart Air Force Base, Tennessee, at the government's price. Ralph Luttrell, then section chief, has admitted that he had drafted an official letter to Internal Revenue, pointing out "the possibility of tax evasion" in the Carmack case. The builder was subjected to intensive investigation, which ended in dismissal of fraud charges against him. One high official even used the Internal Revenue Service to get revenge against a driver whose car bumped his Cadillac at the Washington National Airport. The official copied the license number of the other car, traced the owner's identity, then secured an investigation into his taxes.

More than one hardpressed taxpayer has found himself in trouble because of a trivial or unintentional error in an old return, the failure of an employer to withhold the correct tax, or a personal tragedy which cleaned him out of the money he had set aside for Uncle Sam. The files are stuffed with complaints from taxpayers who say they have been hounded, bullied, and browbeaten by collectors whose methods would put a loan shark to shame.

Uncle Sam's aim is to be firm but fair with all taxpayers. Rich and poor are supposed to be equal in the sharp eye of the IRS, which tries to administer the tax laws without regard for social standing or political pull. Yet policy and practice don't always coincide. Often tax settlements are reached by a process about as equitable as a medieval trial by fire and water. The rich man has recourse to lawyers and experts who can find loopholes in the law or stall a case in the courts. Since Uncle Sam loses almost half the cases that are tried, sometimes he settles for what the court would likely award. This saves legal costs which whittle away the money Internal Revenue is trying to collect.

Chairman Wilbur Mills of the House Ways and Means Committee, which writes the nation's tax laws, appointed a panel of 22 prominent tax attorneys and accountants to investigate how the laws are being administered. The group found many acts of "overzealousness" which had infringed "the vital rights and dignities" of individuals. Treasury's claims that these acts were outside official policy was disingenuous.

Not all bureaucracy is reprehensible. Peeping out from under one of Parkinson's laws ("Subordinates multiply at a fixed rate, regardless of the amount of work produced.") is an agency in contradiction. It consists of three nondescript men, all wearing rumpled suits and the expressions of husbands who are nagged by their wives. They know more about prostitution than anyone else in America. Under federal contract, they are conducting a quiet survey of prostitution that began in 1912. The three have a total of 75 years in America's bordellos, seedy cafes and skid row streets. Their petticoat espionage has pinpointed prostitution centers for public health and law enforcement agencies.

The three-man team has reported that the silk-and-marble pleasure palaces are dying out, that the crime syndicates have turned from vice to more profitable enterprises and that, as a result, prostitution is becoming disorganized. The five worst prostitution cities today, according to the secret reports are: New York (particularly the Times Square area), San Francisco, Seattle, Louisville, and Washington, D.C.

The federally-funded prostitution study was uncovered by newsmen in an obscure government listing, which referred to a public health service grant for a "survey of commercialized prostitution." This was listed — honest — under the heading, "U.S. Government Procurements."

The American Social Health Association, which supervises the three-man team, at first begged news media to keep its 57-year secret inviolate. It finally agreed to a story on the promise that the three agents would be identified only by their code initials — P.K., W.H., and U.L. W.H. and U.L. are known to the association staff itself only by these code letters. Both married, they spend some 10 months out of each year on the road. P.K. is their supervisor.

The P-squad goes into a city only when it is invited by a civil or social agency. In Chicago or New York, they spend a month; in smaller towns, a week. Before they leave town, the city fathers know where prostitutes work, how much they earn, how many there are, who the madams and panders are and whether the trade is dying or flourishing. The agents also learn who in government is in cahoots with the daughters of the game and what the ties are to organized crime. P.K. was almost beaten to death by the Capone gang in 1933 on Wabash Street after he turned up 240 houses of prostitution during the Chicago World's Fair.

Now in his 70s, P.K. has been on the P-squad for 50 years. He spoke to a newsman by telephone from an undisclosed point arranged by the association. The old-style bordellos, he said, have been virtually wiped out. This has taken the profit out of prostitution for the Mafia which, he added, has all but dropped prostitution as a sideline. "The Mafia wants more money than they can make in prostitution now." P.K. said. "It's too disorganized for them, not like it was in the days of (Lucky) Luciano. In a town of 250,000 now, we don't expect to find more than two bordellos and those open just a few scheduled hours a day. In the old days, there would be 10, 15 women in a house. Now it's one or two." The vogue now, he said, "is street walkers, call girls, party girls."

The five cities mentioned in his reports as the worst have been surveyed in the last six months. Some may have begun to clean up. But in New York, he said, "streetwalking has never been worse."

The three men work separately, talking with hotel bellmen and cabdrivers, interviewing streetwalkers, call girls, madams and procurers. Sometimes the agents pose as customers, sometimes as members of kindred rackets. P.K. is adept at the look of half-shame and half-daring that brings on a proposition as quickly as it does to his younger aides, one in his early 40's, the other in his late 50's. All have also developed a strong resistance for the temptation of the job.

There is good reason for their ability to win the confidences of the underworld of sex. Unlike local vice squad members, they have unfamiliar faces. They don't make arrests or testify. Their sole aim is to gather facts so detailed and reliable that they match FBI investigation. The secret reports go to the FBI, Defense Department, Public Health Service and other government agencies which request them. Internal Revenue may request a specific report, for instance, when it is investigating unreported income.

In the last 50 years, the P-squads have visited 15,000 communities. During World War II, the squad grew to 12 men. But since then, as the agents swooped down on one red light district after another, the prostitution houses have cleaned up. Now the team numbers three, a victim of its own success.

JUDICIARY

The Supreme Court of the United States is referred to more and more often in recent years as "those nine cantankerous old men." That's mainly because its most recent decisions have been deeply split and each dissension waspishly written.

The country was forewarned of this conflict when President Nixon, in his inaugural speech, set top priority on changing the complexion of the High Court. He felt that the Court's decisions over recent years had created a permissive atmosphere which had encouraged the spread of crime in the nation. To remedy this, he appointed Warren Burger to be Chief Justice, thus producing an ideological conflict that has led to the dissension felt within the Court and manifest in its decisions.

Fortunately or not, depending on the point of view, Supreme Court decisions flow from the majority of the moment and so every President, from George Washington on, has tried to stack the federal judiciary with as many of "his kind" of justices as possible. This generally meant with men from the President's own political party. The practice, once it was begun by Washington, has been adhered to through the years, so that today only two of the fourteen men who have served as Chief Justice were appointed by Presidents who belonged to a political party different from the appointee's. This fact leads to the often voiced belief that Supreme Court justices, bouyed by the immense dignity and responsibility of the office, rise above their party strictures and render decisions in collusion with the gods. Generally speaking, this is not true. A justice has more often than not been beholden to the President who appointed him and has—again, generally—rewarded his patron with the type of decisions expected of him, that is, with decisions that were in harmony with the traditions and interests of his own party. It is, however, interesting if not encouraging to note that all nine members of the Supreme Court of the early 1950's had been appointed by Democrats. And it was the most divided court in the nation's history.

To the public, today's nine black-robed Justices appear agreeable enough in their leather chairs behind the magnificent mahogany bench. But in the backrooms, they have been behaving like cranky old men. Affable Earl Warren, the former Chief Justice, was able to keep peace among the strong personalities on the nation's highest court. But his successor, Chief Justice Warren Burger, lacks the finesse.

Their private sessions, say insiders, are stiffly formal. Burger expresses his opinion followed, in turn, by the other Justices according to seniority. After the discussion, Burger decides who should write the decisions and sends the assignments on a printed list to each member of the court. The bickering and backbiting is confined largely to their private chambers. The word has leaked out of Burger's chambers, for instance, that the Chief Justice considers Justice William O. Douglas a discredit to the court.

Some Associate Justices have an equally low opinion of Burger whose arbitrary, sometimes arrogant, ways annoy them. They compare him unfavorably to the retired Earl Warren. Douglas, in private, attributes Warren's superior handling of the court to his political skill. He had an understanding of the nation's social, economic and political problems that went beyond the letter of the law, says Douglas.

Shortly before Warren's appointment in 1953, the nine Justices discussed the school segregation issue behind closed doors. They were split 5 to 4 in favor of continuing segregation. But Chief Justice Fred Vinson died and was replaced by Warren before a public decision was reached. Insiders recall that the new Chief Justice quietly began to persuade his colleagues to change their view. He wrote out his own strong opinion against segregation in longhand and delivered it personally to each member of the court. He combined this with a gentle private appeal.

One by one, Justices Felix Frankfurter, Hugo Black, Tom Clark and Stanley Reed—all of whom had signified behind closed doors that they would vote for continued segregation—switched sides. The last to agree was Justice Robert Jackson, who was hospitalized. Warren took his opinion to the·hospital to explain it personally to Jackson. The verdict against segregation, to the astonishment of the nation, was unanimous. Later, Warren used the same soft sell to get another unexpected 7 to 2 decision requiring state legislatures to reapportion on a one-man, one-vote basis.

In contrast, Burger has been getting highly fragmented decisions out of his colleagues on the bench, as public evidence of the internal discord.

The new Chief Justice takes pride in his stern, legalistic view of the Constitution. But insiders recall that Earl Warren, who was bitterly denounced by the strict constructionists, always carried a copy of the Constitution with him wherever he went. They also remember Warren's rueful commentary. "The Founding Fathers," they quote him as saying, "managed to compress the entire blueprint for our government into 5,000 words. They did a magnificent job. But if we had to write the Constitution over today, we would probably fail. The lobbies and pressure groups are too strong."

The fact is, that since Warren Burger took over as Chief Justice, it has become harder and harder to tell the Supreme Court from King Arthur's Court.

The redoubtable Chief Justice, with his pompadoured white mane combed back and his black robe flowing, may not be the court's best legal scholar, but he's tops in handsomeness and high-handedness. For example, not long after joining the court, he annexed to his personal offices the conference room, the inner sanctum where the Justices meet in secret to thrash out their decisions. He even installed a desk so there could be no mistaking that the court convenes in Burger's lair. The Chief Justice also has a length of gold carpet rolled out for the august jurists to cross as they make their way through a rear hallway to take their seats on the bench.

Not surprisingly, the court's budget requests are on the rise. In 1971, the Burger court asked for nearly 20 per cent more money than it had received the year before. Among the requested items were $5,000 to give the Chief Justice a budget for entertaining for the first time in history, another $8,000 for automatic floor-cleaning equipment. It would be unfair to say that Burger is being stingy with the grandeur—he also asked Congress for $6,000 to rent cars for all the other justices for the first time.

Such requests do not normally meet enthusiastic approval from the tight-fisted curmudgeons who head the House appropriations subcommittees. But Burger—like previous chief justices—did no. stoop to appear before them to explain his budget. In his place he sent Potter Stewart and Byron (Whizzer) White, who got the accustomed going over by Brooklyn's John Rooney, one of Congress' irascible geezers. Told by Stewart that the Chief Justice had already spent $2,000 from his own pocket for entertaining, Rooney snapped, "Well, I daresay there is not a member of Congress who does not spend far in excess of $2,000 a year to entertain the people who call upon him... What is the salary of the Chief Justice, and does he not get an automobile and a chauffeur?"

"His salary is $62,500 and he does get an automobile and a chauffeur," replied Stewart.

"And he could not absorb this," pressed Rooney.

"I am sure he could absorb it, Mr. Chairman, as he has," conceded Stewart.

But even more disturbing than Burger's silly pursuit of baronial splendor, are the signs that the Chief Justice may be a jurist of severely limited abilities. During the historic court clash between the government and *The New York Times* and the *Baltimore Post,* Burger asked some questions that indicated he didn't know what was going on. At one point he reminded *The Washington Post* lawyer, William Glendon, that the *Post* apparently acquired the famous "Pentagon Papers" by illicit means. He then brought up an old legal doctrine that frowns upon anyone's seeking redress from a court ("coming into equity" is the legal expression) when his own hands are not clean.

Glendon patiently informed the Chief Justice that the *Post* had not "come into equity" but had been brought in "kicking and screaming" by the government. Later, Burger was informed that both newspapers had refused to produce the documents in their possession because they felt it might give away their source. The press' right to protect its sources is a major constitutional question that at the time was to be ruled on by the High Court in the following Fall session. Burger, however, seemed oblivious to this. He acted shocked when he heard that the lower courts in the *Times-Post* case had upheld them in refusing to produce the papers. "He let that (the constitutional question) override federal rules of civil procedure on discovery?" Burger blurted.

Not even the most shallow federal judge would take the view that a constitutional right is less important than the federal rules of procedure. But Burger apparently thinks they are.

SENATE REJECTS

The Senate, of course, must approve presidential appointees to the Supreme Court, and it's a rare occasion when it doesn't. It is even rarer for the Senate to reject two candidates in succession. It has done this only twice: the first time was in 1894, during the second Cleveland Administration; the other spanned 1969 and 1970 of the Nixon Administration.

Clement F. Haynsworth, Jr. of South Carolina was nominated by President Nixon on August 18, 1969, to fill the associate justice seat left vacant by the resignation that May of Abe Fortas. (Fortas, a Johnson appointee, quit under fire, thus setting the stage for a burning

controversy over judicial ethics that would give the double rejection of
Nixon's nominees an almost vengeful cast.) The Senate refused to
confirm Haynsworth the following November with a 44-55 roll-call vote.
The opposition had rekindled the controversy ignited when Fortas was
accused of accepting an outside fee from the family foundation of a
convicted stock manipulator. Opponents of the nomination said
repeatedly that they were not questioning Haynsworth's honesty or
integrity, but rather his sensitivity to the appearance of ethical
impropriety and his judgment regarding participation in cases where his
financial interests were involved. He was also opposed by labor and civil
rights leaders. But he was the President's choice to reinforce the tone of
the evolving "Nixon Court," a tone set by the choice of Warren E. Burge
as Chief Justice. Haynsworth was regarded as fitting Nixon's definitior
of a "strict Constitutional constructionist."

   Following the Senate action, Nixon issued a statement of regret and
continued support for the jurist. "An outstanding jurist," he said, "who
would have brought great credit to the Supreme Court...has been
rejected by the...Senate. I deeply regret this action. I believe a majority of
people in the nation regret it." But the President was merely playing ouᵗ
to the end his pledge to Republican congressional leaders that he would
stand behind Haynsworth "even if he gets only one vote." In a closed-
door session before the vote was taken, Nixon showed a stubborn streak
by standing firm against the nearly unanimous counsel of his
congressional advisers that it would be more prudent politics to
withdraw Haynsworth's nomination. The President, apparently
referring to his Democratic critics, snorted, "They will attack all my
appointments to the court." He shrugged off charges that Haynsworth's
holdings constituted a conflict of interest, noting that "six present
justices own securities."

   Texas Sen. John Tower, the Senate Republican campaign chairman,
wanted to be sure that the White House wouldn't buckle under the
political pressure. When the President stepped briefly out of the room,
Tower told Vice President Agnew he could get more support for
Haynsworth "if assurance can be given of no retreat from the
nomination."

   "Only the President can answer that," said Agnew. "I know how he
feels. I know how I feel."

   Tower put the question to Nixon when he returned: Was there any
possibility that the White House would drop the nomination or that
Haynsworth would withdraw? The President turned to Attorney General
John Mitchell for the answer.

   "Haynsworth has no disposition to withdraw," said the Attorney
General. "To do so would reflect upon his ability to sit where he is now."

"Perhaps judges should not own stock," the President suggested to the closed-door conference. He discussed his own assets, acknowledged that the ethical question can be "troublesome" but insisted that Haynsworth "has followed the laws of the land." Nixon also called him "the best judge in his age group," then delivered an impassioned little speech to the party leaders.

"I hold in my hands the fate of the man," declared the President. "I will not be a party to destroying the man. Unless some new fact comes in, I will stick by Haynsworth even if he gets only one vote. Will I withdraw him? I will not!"

Both of the administration's Senate chieftains, GOP leader Hugh Scott of Pennsylvania and assistant leader Robert Griffin of Michigan, earlier had urged him to withdraw Haynsworth's nomination to the Supreme Court. As early as September 30 Griffin reported to the President behind closed White House doors that the prospects for Haynsworth's confirmation looked grim. Scott soberly confirmed the report. Even Senator Tower, a staunch Haynsworth booster, expressed reservations, according to the confidential minutes, over Haynsworth's business conflicts. But the President, recalling how he had overcome the opposition to the close-fought antiballistic missile program, was supremely confident. He felt certain, in the clinches, that he could get Haynsworth confirmed.

He repeated his determination to fight for Haynsworth, no holds barred, at another strategy session on October 14. He brought in Clark Mollenhoff, a former investigative reporter with the *Des Moines Register and Tribune*, to summarize his investigation of Haynsworth's alleged conflicts. Mollenhoff reviewed six cases and concluded that the analogy to Justice Abe Fortas, who resigned from the Supreme Court over conflicts, was "nonexistent." The President said he had "checked" the ethical question with Mollenhoff. The confidential minutes then quote Nixon as declaring, "On the qualifications, I'm for (Haynsworth). On these ethical problems, all these problems are troublesome. Some objections are ideological, some sectional, some go to his judgment."

In the end, the President decided to override the advice of his Senate leaders. He subsequently acknowledged to subordinates that he had made a mistake and that, thereafter, he would listen more closely to them.

The President blamed Senator Ted Kennedy, above all others, for the Haynsworth defeat. The Senate GOP leaders reported to the President that Kennedy was the real backstage leader of the Democratic dissidents, that Kennedy had deliberately dragged out the Haynsworth hearings to increase the embarrassment to the Nixon Administration and that Kennedy had indeed become the chief obstacle to the Administration's moves in the Senate.

MITCHELL CALLED THE TUNE

Astounded Senators soon learned that Supreme Court nominee Haynsworth's testimony before the Senate Judiciary Committee had actually been prepared for him by the man who arranged his appointment in the first place—Attorney General John Mitchell. Indeed, Haynsworth's opening statement was all typed and ready for him to deliver before he ever reached Washington. After his arrival, he cloistered himself at the Justice Department to study the words that Mitchell had prepared for him. Senators carefully verified that the statement had been prepared by Mitchell, not Haynsworth. If Mitchell had such influence .hat he literally could put words in Haynsworth's mouth, Senators wondered whether Mitchell would also be able to dictate Haynsworth decisions on the high court.

Note: When Senators demanded Haynsworth's financial records, the Justice Department concealed the fact that they were readily available at the department, not in scattered places as the public was led to believe. Mitchell's men were studying them feverishly to see whether the judge had forgotten to tell them about other inept mixing of his financial and judicial roles.

THE CARSWELL DEBACLE

So much for Haynsworth. Now Nixon began looking for someone else to fill the Fortas seat on the High Court and accordingly on January 19, 1970, he placed before the Senate the name of G. Harold Carswell of Florida, a Judge with the Fifth Circuit Court of Appeals. And the lightning struck twice. On April 8 the Senate dealt Nixon his second major defeat when it rejected Carswell by a roll-call vote of 45-51.

The opposition in this case was slower to mount, mostly because the Senators weren't anxious for another bitter confirmation struggle. It was only with the persistent opposition of Edward W. Brooke (R-Mass.) that other Senators began to feel that Carswell's record was such that he could not be permitted to sit on the High Court. So adamant was Brooke, the only Negro in the Senate, that he paid two private calls upon President Nixon to urge him to withdraw the nomination. Brooke bluntly told the President that Carswell's opponents had enough votes to send the nomination back to the Judiciary Committee where it would remain. However, the President, as we have seen, was taking his advice from Attorney General Mitchell, who at that time advised that should Carswell be rejected, the President ought not make another appointment, but instead take the issue to the people.

After the defeat, Nixon appeared to have taken Mitchell's counsel when he issued a statement saying he had concluded that the Senate as "presently constituted" would never confirm a nominee to the Supreme Court "from the South who believes as I do in the strict construction of the Constitution. . . . As long as the Senate is constituted the way it is today, I will not nominate another Southerner and let him be subjected to the kind of malicious character assassination accorded both Judges Haynsworth and Carswell."

It is clear now that the campaign to confirm Carswell was directed behind the scenes by Attorney General Mitchell, who seems to have been regarded by President Nixon as a political master, but whose campaigns invariably have wound up in near disaster. He ran Nixon's presidential campaign starting with a 16 per cent margin over Hubert Humphrey. By election night Nixon's lead had been whittled down to less than one per cent. It was also Mitchell who directed the confirmation battle for Judge Clement Haynsworth who started out with a clear majority and ended up rejected by the Senate. Under Mitchell's handling, Carswell's majority evaporated completely. Carswell's opponents kept the debate going until the Easter vacation. This gave the Senators a chance to return to their states and find out how the homefolks felt about Carswell. And they discovered surprising opposition. By the time they returned they had enough votes to defeat Carswell.

PORTRAIT OF A JUSTICE

Supreme Court Justice William O. Douglas was threatened with impeachment in 1970. He had been married four times, the last two times to women young enough to have been his granddaughters, and he had published some personal opinions in a less-than-scholarly magazine. He had made a lot of enemies in his 35 years in politics, one of whom may have kept him from being President of the United States. For the fact is, Douglas might have become President in 1945 except for a transposition of names.

At the 1944 Democratic convention, Douglas was neatly maneuvered out of the nomination that put Harry Truman in line for the White House. President Franklin D. Roosevelt had told party leaders at a July 11 dinner before the convention that Truman should be dropped from consideration as the vice presidential candidate if he had reached his 60th birthday. FDR called for a congressional directory which would have revealed that Truman had turned 60 two months earlier. But Bob Hannegan, the Democratic national chairman, favored Truman as a more dependable party man, and slyly contrived to distract Roosevelt's attention from the directory after it had been brought.

A few days later, Roosevelt dictated a letter to the Chicago Convention, saying he would be "glad to go with either" Douglas or Truman. Grace Tully, the president's personal secretary, told Douglas afterward that his name had been listed ahead of Truman's, but that Hannegan had intercepted the letter and retyped it for release with Truman's name first. Thus the press and public got the idea that Truman was FDR's favorite, and the convention carried out history accordingly. This knowledge of how close he came to the presidency, a close friend has said, "has ground at Douglas all these years."

He would never have dropped the atomic bomb on women and children but would have found some other way to impress the Japanese warlords with its power. From the first, he opposed the hard line against China. He was in touch with Red Chinese leaders who persuaded him that they had no desire to be dominated by Russia. Douglas still remains convinced that timely and friendly recognition of Red China not only would have kept the Chinese neutral but would have avoided two decades of crises in Asia, including both the Korean and Vietnam wars.

The ruggedly dignified jurist once explained how he had tried in vain to press his views upon President Truman. Douglas praised Truman's courage and character but complained that "he had no understanding of foreign affairs. He would walk over to the globe and give me a grade school lesson in history. He would point out who were the good guys and who were the bad guys."

Douglas' colleagues on the High Court speak of him with esteem and affection — and perhaps a trace of sorrow. His rugged individualism was forged, they suggest, in the snowy mountains and wild rivers of his native Washington State. He came to know poverty and fear and, with an idealist's fervor, wanted to rid the world of them.

"I suspect," Justice Hugo Black has written, "that he must have come into this world with a rush and that his first cry must have been a protest against something he saw at a glance was wrong or unjust." Justice Abe Fortas has described Douglas even more poignantly as a man with "strength rooted in sensitivity, freedom founded upon struggle, and compassion emerging from pain."

But there is sadness, too, at the Supreme Court over Douglas' publicized marital difficulties. After his fourth marriage, outraged cries rose from the ladies' sewing circles across the land and reverberated on Capitol Hill. No less than four resolutions were introduced calling for a congressional investigation into his "moral character." Only a few supporters, such as the influential *Washington Post*, reminded Congressmen that marriage was a private matter and that Douglas was still performing his judicial duties "with honor and dedication." The verdict might have come from Douglas himself, who in his rulings has championed individual rights. But the critics refused to look beyond his romantic life into the brilliant career of a great libertarian who joined the nation's highest court at age 40. He holds seniority and has written about 800 highly respected opinions.

The financial cost of three divorce settlements added to the pressures on a man who yearns to be free of the encumbrances of civilization. The squeeze finally forced him to hire an aggressive agent to sell his writings and to promote his lectures (which opponents find reprehensible). The bad publicity distressed him but he has said, "After 33 years in politics, I've developed a good set of callouses."

Now the white-haired old judge with the youthful spirit is seeking his elusive goal of happiness with his fourth wife. Regularly they retreat out of the glare of public life to the mountain-ringed wilderness where, Douglas once wrote, "a man can find deep solitude and under conditions of grandeur that are startling, he can come to know both himself and God."

CIVIL LIBERTIES

Words like "socialist", "communist", "fascist" don't really mean anything these days, so it's fruitless — academically — to insist on pigeonholing the world along those lines. For the world has evolved and can no longer be classified with political jargon out of another age.

A nation today is likely to be operating under a system of government that incorporates a dash of all the above ingredients, so if one feels a compulsion to classify nations for easy and casual reference, he ought to come up with a new device. One such device might be to divide the nations in terms of the civil liberties each grants its citizens. The listings, to be sure, would be different and truer to life.

Russia, for instance, in the lexicon of the 19th Century is a communist or socialist state; America is imperialist. But by using the civil liberties filing system, it becomes quite clear that Mother Russia is appallingly more repressive of civil freedoms than is, say, Sweden or the Netherlands; indeed, it becomes strikingly apparent that ideologically she functions a good deal like a classic military dictatorship. And since military dictatorship is the heavy water of fascism, one has little choice but to file Russia under "fascist" states.

And if the true difference between nations is how free the people are to function within the society, then the United States must be ranked in almost polar opposition to Russia — which places us just about where the Establishment (God bless us) has always said we were. For this nation surely ranks high in civil liberties. Not the highest perhaps; the system isn't perfect, certainly.

It isn't perfect because business, industry and government so often suffer from a messiah complex, which induces business and industry to fix prices and deny citizens the right to free enterprise; the government to spend its energies spying and compiling dossiers on private citizens. It is a sorry commentary to say that one of the highest ranking nations in terms of civil liberties spies on its people. But it's true. And it's unnecessary.

Most government agencies traffic in information about the sexual habits, financial affairs, personal friendships, political and religious beliefs of job applicants. The Defense Department alone has accumulated more than 14 million life histories in the course of its security investigations. These are loaded with derogatory comments — true statements, deliberate lies, idle gossip — whispered into the ears of eager agents.

The Civil Service Commission keeps in its secret files another 8 million dossiers on people who have applied for federal jobs. These files hold the darkest secrets of many persons who may have at some time in their pasts committed improper or questionable acts.

Even the Federal Housing Administration receives confidential reports on the marital stability of prospective home buyers. The purpose is to spot couples who are likely to get divorced and may no longer keep up their house payments.

The General Services Administration maintains a blacklist of businessmen who are considered poor business risks. It is possible to get on this select list without ever committing a provable offense.

Then, of course, the FBI is constantly checking into the backgrounds of people for one purpose or another. It has on file an astounding 200 millions sets of fingerprints, not to mention dossiers on tens of thousands of suspected communists, security risks and crooks.

It is no secret that the FBI also keeps files on controversial figures suspected of nothing more incriminating than speaking their own mind. The FBI submitted a report to former President Lyndon Johnson, for example, on the sex life of the late Dr. Martin Luther King. A secret report, dated February 20, 1968, by a White House aide, was devoted entirely to a titillating account of an alleged love affair — a matter that was no business of the FBI nor the White House.

The dirt that government gumshoes pick up on people is swept into dossiers which are freely exchanged between federal offices. When the State Department is asked to watch the movements of an overseas traveler for instance, the raw charges against him are distributed to at least four offices.

The traffic in unproved allegations is shockingly promiscuous. Not only are the dossiers widely circulated, but most of them carry a low security classification. This gives an alarming number of government employees access to derogatory information about fellow citizens.

A certain small formality is required before Internal Revenue will show tax returns to outside agencies. But the red tape is routine, the access easy. The only real rule seems to be that the sleuths should be careful not to tip off the taxpayer. The IRS has issued strict instructions that "the taxpayer should be given no indication that the national office or other federal agency is interested in this matter."

The tax returns of every presidential appointee are carefully checked before his appointment is approved. This practice was started in 1961 by the late President Kennedy after two of his appointees, the late James Landis and Frank Reeves, turned out to be tax delinquents.

In the case of presidential appointees, however, the raw returns aren't turned over to the FBI. The IRS merely summarizes the tax information on what is called a Type X report.

Not even the mails, apparently, are inviolate. Almost any agency can ask the Post Office for a mail check to find out who's writing to whom.

Federal snoops have even been caught poking into people's garbage. A few years back, a Washington woman happened to notice through the window that her trash was segregated and hauled away in a burlap bag. After it happened twice she made inquiries that led to an investigation. It turned out that the garbage collectors of the District of Columbia have a list of 50 persons whose trash was set aside and delivered in burlap bags to a special room in a government building. Here unidentified men would come in the night to spirit away the bags for scrutiny. It was explained that the trash was segregated "to determine from typical household units the characteristics of refuse for statistical and design purpose." It was left unanswered, however, why the trash for this solemn study should be collected only from people about whom some official agencies had a special curiosity.

Unsuspecting Americans may be closer to George Orwell's concept of 1984 than they may think. Orwell described an advanced police state whose citizens couldn't make a move without Big Brother knowing it. For some time, our federal uncle has been developing a Big Brother complex. He may not be watching everyone at the moment, but he can concentrate an infinite variety of eyes and ears — electronic, mechanical and human — on anyone who stirs his suspicion.

In the not-too-distant future, both the spying devices and intrusive interrogations may be brought together in eternal union. That day, which could extinguish forever the right of privacy, may come if the government approves existing studies for a national data center. The idea, still vague in its specifics, is to set up a computerized master file on all Americans. All-knowing, never-forgetting electronic machines, crammed with all the information ever divulged by or pried from private citizens, could produce at the press of a button a person's life record from cradle to grave, complete with distortions built-in.

Advocates of this idea claim that a master file could provide the government with speedy and accurate information needed to solve national problems. They say the data would be used for statistical reference, not personal prying. Yet the very existence of such a computer file would encourage fact-finders to introduce ever more revealing questionnaires.

CHANGE UNLIKELY

Can the snoopers be stopped? Congressional champions of privacy are not optimistic. They have repeatedly confronted investigative agencies with evidence of illegal snooping, but the agencies usually deny it, always get away with it, and don't seem to care about the legal questions. Since wiretaps are intended to pick up leads rather than evidence, they don't care whether the information is legally admissible in court.

Indignant Congressmen have pressured the Defense Department into giving fewer lie detector tests, but many are still given. They have convinced other agencies to make the intrusive psychological tests voluntary, but these, too, are still wide-spread.

The federal government's 2.8 million employees, in particular, feel the presence of Big Brother. They found a champion in Sen. Sam Ervin (D-N.C.) who declared, "Psychological testing, psychiatric interviews, race questionnaires, lie detectors, loyalty oaths, probing personal forms and background investigations, restrictions on communicating with Congress, pressure to support political parties financially, yet restrictions on all other political activity, coercion to buy savings bonds, extensive limitations on outside activities, rules for speaking and writing and even thinking, forms for revealing personal data about finances, creditors, property and other interests — all of these increasingly shrink the realm of personal liberty and violate individual privacy."

The 18-year-old daughter of an Army colonel applied for a summer job with the State Department. She had interim secret clearance because she had worked for the department the previous summer. Nevertheless, she was subjected to a four-hour grilling. The personal probe got around to the subject of a boy she had dated. Then her interrogators fired these questions at her: "Did he abuse you? Did he do anything unnatural with you? There's kissing, petting and intercourse, and after that did he force you to do anything to him, or did he do anything to you?" A top official later said the cross-examination was a "uniform policy."

One veteran civil servant, angry about a financial-disclosure form, summed up the feelings of those who believe tough new laws are needed to protect individual rights. He complained that the government seemed all too eager for "information that can be of no practical value to anyone except some bureaucrat determined to establish a Big Brother complex. In many seemingly innocuous but prying little ways, the government is compiling data on each one of us which can lead to a highly regimented society reminiscent of Stalin's Russia, Hitler's Germany, Mussolini's Italy, to name a few."

JEOPARDY ASSESSMENT

One of the most insidious federal weapons is the jeopardy assessment, which is supposed to be used to tie up the funds of taxpayers who might try to skip the country. Agents have used this power indiscriminately to force settlements out of reluctant taxpayers. In Missouri, one agent barged into a bank with a $2.35 assessment on a businessman's account, though the agent could have collected the money merely by calling on the businessman a few doors down the street.

Noel Smith, a farmer in Taylor, Missouri, had his funds tied up for four years after he refused to pay a $570,000 tax claim. He was obliged to live off the proceeds of a business deal in Canada. The government finally offered to settle the claim for less than 10 cents on the dollar. Though he stoutly insisted he didn't owe anything, he coughed up $54,000 in order to get access to his own bank account again. He complained that the four-year ordeal had ruined his reputation, broken his health and cost him $1 million in lost profits. "If I had it to do over again," he said, "it would be easier to go to jail."

Several government contractors complained to the press that some agencies have become obsessed with audits and investigations. They have seized upon technical violations and treated respectable businessmen like criminals. In a case that has become all too typical, the Court of Claims recently "lectured" a federal contracting official for his arrogance and arbitrariness. "He nearly took a shillelagh and struck the contractor down," declared the court.

CONTRACTORS SQUEEZED

For many contractors without political influence, government profits are no longer worth the harassment. More than one has said he would never bid on a government contract again. A top General Services Administration official said he couldn't blame them. "We're fighting with every contractor we do business with," he said wearily.

Frequently Uncle Sam holds up payment until the contractor, desperate for money to meet his bills, settles for less than he was supposed to get. One contractor, in order to rush work on the Bomarc missile, lived for four months in a trailer and worked around the clock at the missile site. But the government was in no such rush to pay him. Eight years after the contract was completed, he was still trying to collect what was due him. Worse, Uncle Sam doesn't hesitate to use criminal charges to coerce a contractor into accepting a civil settlement. "You will find," said an attorney, "that a fraud investigation almost always follows civil dispute." S. Harvey Klein, a Philadelphia electronics manufacturer, got into a legal hassle with the government over the termination of a contract. Not until he had rejected the government's settlement offer did he find himself under investigation for allegedly filing a false claim.

The Brussel Sewing Machine Co. had a government contract reviewed by the Renegotiation Board, which concluded that the company's profits had not been excessive. After the case was closed an informer charged that the company had overstated its estimated cost. Investigators immediately swarmed all over the company, and the government filed a false-claim charge. The court, however, was unimpressed with the government's arguments, and concluded that it was not "the intention of the statute (governing such contracts) to make dealing with the government hazardous, should someone later conceive the notion that the government had paid too much."

John A. Maxwell, a Michigan manufacturer, was actually fined $30,000 and sentenced to a three-year prison term because he had followed the government's own suggestion and filed estimated instead of exact costs. It had been agreed that the exact figure would be determined later. Though the government had been a party to his act, it brought criminal charges against him for submitting estimated, hence "false," figures. The Appeals Court found the government's position so outrageous that it set aside the guilty verdict.

BUGGING THE GOVERNORS

Every instance cited here is a blatant, arbitrary treading on the citizen's civil liberties. There are other examples. No one is immune; not even governors of most of the United States. The most confidential conversations of the nation's governors can be overheard at any point along an emergency telephone system that links their private offices with Civil Defense headquarters.

It was discovered recently that the red emergency telephones in most governors' offices have been transformed into secret listening devices. The microphone in each receiver will pick up conversations in the room when the telephone is on the hook. Reporters personally listened to a conversation that an electronics expert, using simple wiretap tools, easily picked up in the office of Maryland's Governor Marvin Mandel. The conversation was transmitted through the emergency telephone under the governor's desk.

An estimated 30 governors have similar telephones that have been rigged for eavesdropping. These insidious telephones connect into a hotline, which enables Civil Defense to have instant communications with the governors in a national crisis. The hotline, referred to in classified documents as "The Special Service Line for Civil Defense," is supposed to be strictly hush-hush. It is difficult, therefore, to get any official information. From unofficial but reliable sources, however, the "Washington Merry-Go-Round" column was able to establish the following facts:

The emergency telephones were installed about 15 years ago as part of a secret network whose main terminal is located in Colorado Springs. The network links most governors, who can be called simultaneously in case of an emergency.

The receivers were wired in such a way that they can pick up everything said in the governors' offices. Some officials insist the wiring was an "innocent mistake." But electronics experts say flatly there was no possibility of a mistake. They say the telephones must have been deliberately rigged to eavesdrop on the governors.

Secrecy is used to cover up the identity of those responsible for transforming the governors' telephones into hidden mikes. Some officials say the telephones were wired by the American Telephone and Telegraph Company. Others say the rigging was done by the federal government. AT&T would make no comment, except to say all information would have to come from the customers.

Even more mysterious is the identity of the listeners. Some think it must be the FBI. Others say the CIA is the most likely culprit.

Governor Mandel was the first to discover his emergency telephone was bugged. He angrily summoned telephone officials and demanded to know who was responsible. Reporters got wind of his protests and questioned him, and he confirmed that an electronics specialist had checked the red telephone under his desk and found it was wired to pick up every sound in the room.

He said his predecessor, Spiro Agnew, had discovered a hidden mike in the governor's office before moving up to the vice presidency. As a result, Mandel began checking the office regularly for mikes and wiretaps after he moved in. The red emergency telephone had been ignored, he said, on the assumption that the secret hotline must be secure. But later, a new electronics expert insisted upon checking it and demonstrated how the emergency telephone functioned as a secret transmitter.

Outraged, he called in the telephone people and made other confidential inquiries. He said the telephone officials not only acknowledged that his special telephone was bugged but said all emergency telephones were wired the same way. This would mean all the governors on the hotline had bugged telephones, they told him. Mandel could hardly believe it. To satisfy himself, he arranged to send an electronics specialist to check the emergency telephone of a neighboring governor. Mandel said the governor, whom he declined to identify, was also shocked to find how the telephone transmitted all the conversations in the office

Meanwhile Mandell ordered the microphone removed from his emergency telephone. He said the telephone had never rung during his 22 months as governor and probably hadn't been used since it was installed. But the day after he removed the microphone, the telephone rang. He happened to be out of the office, but his personal secretary, Grace Donald, confirmed that there had been six short, sharp rings on the emergency telephone. Since only the governor is supposed to answer the hotline, she didn't pick it up.

Jack Anderson (co-author of this book) asked the governor's permission to tap into the hotline to test for himself whether he could overhear what went on inside his office. Lt. Norval Cooper, a state trooper trained in electronics, was assigned to accompany him. The microphone was screwed back into the emergency telephone, and Cooper used common wiretap tools to plug into the hotline at a nearby switchbox. Every word spoken in the governor's office was distinctly audible. By using a voice-activated recorder, the full conversation could easily have been taped.

MILITARY MEMO

The military being what it is, one shouldn't be surprised to find certain civil freedoms a little ragged from manhandling. Insubordination, for example, is any civilian's prerogative. All he risks is his job. In the military service, however, it's one of the more serious crimes and is harshly dealt with. We have accepted this distortion over the years because the official line is that armies cannot function without instant and thoughtless discipline. (Now, with the uncovering of the My Lai massacre and the subsequent trials, that venerable maxim, too, is being questioned.) Just how far one's civil liberties are brushed aside by the military system perhaps may be measured by an intercorps memo reproduced completely in Figure 1. It is dated Dec. 21, 1970, and is addressed to "all personnel" from the commanding officer:

Figure 1

DISPOSITION FORM
For use of this form, see AR 340-15; the proponent agency is The Adjutant General's Office.

REFERENCE OR OFFICE SYMBOL	SUBJECT
SMUPA	Reporting Items of Intelligence Interest

TO All Personnel	FROM Commanding Officer	DATE 1 Dec 70	CMT 1

1. The Oath of Office taken by each individual appointed to the Federal Service, whether military or civilian, includes a statement that he "will support and defend the Constitution of the United States against all enemies, foreign and domestic." There are many ways in which one may support and defend the Constitution; however, one of the most basic methods is to report to the local Security Officer any incident which could threaten the National Security or cause a disruption of normal government operations.

2. The most obvious threats to our security are those created by foreign intelligence agencies who are constantly seeking to obtain information which we consider worthy of protection. Foreign agents seldom have direct access to classified information; however, too often they have been able to find cleared and trusted employees who will obtain such information for them. Individuals are recruited who have weaknesses in their character or personal habits or who have serious financial difficulties. If these weaknesses are sufficiently obvious to attract the attention of a hostile agent, they must certainly be recognizable to fellow workers. It is imperative that such weaknesses be reported to the Security Office if any action is to be taken to prevent these individuals from becoming vulnerable to exploitation.

3. There is also growing concern for the domestic threat to our National Security. We know that there are many groups and individuals who are creating unrest throughout the country, and some who are actively engaged in attacks on all branches of government. Their actions against federal installations range from distribution of disruptive printed media to destruction of government equipment and facilities. In order to protect lives and government property, it is vital that as much information as possible be collected and studied. I urge each of you to notify the Security Office if you become aware that any individual, organization, or group is engaged in any activity which could threaten the National Security or disrupt government operations. If information is obtained from newspapers, periodicals, or flyers, copies of the items should be provided.

4. Remember, the vigilance of each citizen protects the freedom of all.

W.A. WALKER
Colonel, Ord Corps
Commanding

FORM
DA 1 FEB 62 2496   REPLACES DD FORM 96, EXISTING SUPPLIES OF WHICH WILL BE
                         ISSUED AND USED UNTIL 1 FEB 63 UNLESS SOONER EXHAUSTED.

A SECOND DECLARATION OF DEMOCRACY?

In the light of all these abuses of civil liberties, it has become fashionable to deprecate America, to accept falsehoods about the United States as noble truth, to adopt the "double-speak" and "double-think" that was predicted by Orwell.

Increasingly, fascist dictatorships are accepted as people's democracy; brotherhood, peace, justice — and all they stand for — have been debased in the language mint. Yet this spurious coinage is having an alarmingly successful acceptance among social critics, political reformers, literary intellectuals, questing youths and other concerned Americans.

Here are four leading lies that the double-thinkers have given common currency:

1. *America is a police state.* As evidence, they point accusingly at police abuses, civil rights violations and government eavesdropping. Yet no responsible American really believes the President will use the police, as a dictator would, to keep himself in power. Most police officials stay in their place and remain subservient to the electorate. Indeed, the police are probably overridden more often than they are upheld by our courts. The greater danger is that antipolice attitudes will spread until the police become discredited and lose public support. This would bring the chaos that the revolutionaries seek.

2. *America is imperialistic.* Since World War II, dozens of new nations have been born kicking and squalling, and yelling their defiance. In this revolutionary atmosphere, America has become the symbol of the old order, the status quo, the colonial past. Yet the real imperialists are the fascist powers, which spread their influence through the gun barrel. They prefer low-cost guerrilla warfare, and nations around the world are threatened by insurgents armed with Soviet and Chinese weapons. But the great Communist powers are also capable of naked aggression, as Hungary, Czechoslovakia, India and Tibet have learned. Because the Reds speak the rhetoric of revolution, however, Communist colonialism is soft pedaled by the double-speakers.

3. *America is a racist regime.* Continuing racial discrimination and the Nixon Administration's indifference toward the minorities give some credence to this calumny. But the truth is that America's minorities enjoy more rights and greater prosperity than are found in most countries.

4. *The press is no longer free in America.* Like all governments, Washington officialdom tries to manipulate the flow of information to the people. But the Supreme Court dramatically demonstrated by its 6-to-3 vote against government restraints on *The New York Times* and *The Washington Post* that the press is still free in America. Indeed, the "Washington Merry-Go-Round" syndicated column, critical as it is of the

high and mighty, couldn't be published in most countries. And our underground press isn't underground at all but is free to publish the most revolutionary invective without interference.

NEWS MEDIA AND THE PUBLIC

Most Americans will acknowledge, if pressed, that they are the most enlightened people on earth. There is scarcely a home in the country that doesn't keep its fires blazing in the winter with the late editions. Nowhere else can so many men tell you precisely how many baseballs Willie Mays has slammed over the fence. Only in America are the ladies so steeped in the problems of the lovelorn.

Far fewer men, of course, can tell you how many metal balls have been knocked into outer space or which nation is ahead in the great space race. Fewer women can discuss domestic problems, if these happen to be national rather than marital. And more newspaper readers follow the action in the comic strips than the real thing in Vietnam. Public interest in congressional debates is so low that a legislator simply cannot count upon the voters to re-elect him for championing their cause. All too often, he is obliged to support the pressure groups and special interests, which pay far closer attention to what goes on in Congress. If Americans would concern themselves with tax legislation enough to compel Congress to close the loopholes, for example, they probably could reduce federal income taxes by half.

It has been said that about 80 per cent of the adult population knows next to nothing about foreign affairs. During the Berlin blockade in 1959, for instance, the Survey Research Center found that 37 per cent of the people did not even know of any trouble in Berlin, while a *New York Times* survey showed that many people did not even know that Berlin was located inside East Germany. Another Survey Research Center study conducted in 1964 revealed that 28 per cent of the people interviewed did not know that there was a communist regime in China. Finally, in 1971, the Gallup Poll revealed that only 55 per cent of the people had heard or read about the Pentagon papers revealed by *The New York Times* (and, incidentally, 58 per cent felt the newspapers did right to expose them).

Why are so many people starved for information in a land of plenty, where news is available on the doorstep each morning or at the turn of a television knob? For one thing, they have come to expect their news media to entertain rather than inform. They take their information in small, sugared capsules, scanning the headlines with only half an eye, listening to the news broadcasts with only half an ear. Accordingly, most newspapers serve up the day's events in easy-to-swallow doses. They report who, what, when and where; seldom do they explain why. They reduce great complexities to simplicities. They may sum up a peace-or-war issue in one punchy paragraph or condense a deep debate into a couple of colorful quotes. Most big-city dailies give the public only a sniff of foreign news. Even the local columns are devoted more to police reports, politics, and puffery than to the racial ferment, for instance, that may be about to explode just a few blocks from the editorial rooms. Too few papers dare to print exposes before they are safely recorded in privileged documents or, for that matter, bother to probe behind the daily press handouts.

And if newspapers are guilty, then most radio and television stations are guiltier. Their shining goal is to broadcast enough news to satisfy the Federal Communications Commission that they have performed their public service. "When it comes to covering the news in any kind of detailed way," says television anchorman David Brinkley, "we are just almost not in the ball game." As for radio, 15-minute newscasts have all but disappeared from the air; the surveys show that most listeners get bored after five minutes. This is time for about as much information as could be gleaned from a slow drive past a well-lighted news stand.

Thus, many Americans, underexposed to colorful reality, are left to grope in a subterranean world of half light. It is a bleak world of black and white, of shadows that take on weird, even grotesque shapes. Those who inhabit it become prey for the demagogues. Gullible, they are easily taken in by snap-finger solutions. They accept simple yes-or-no answers, and take comfort from political cure-alls. Nor can they cope with the sophisticated propaganda of the times. The world has been thrust into the age of "double-speak" and "double-think" forecast by the late George Orwell in his farseeing novel, *1984*.

The soapbox patriots are exceeded only by the political pitchmen who would rather exploit than explain issues. They have a language all their own, and it's spoken out of both sides of the mouth. It is a curious double talk, which often accentuates the positive in order to accentuate the negative. They can, in a phrase, defend the indefensible — racial discrimination, say, or war profiteering — in language so lofty as to sound believeable. One must never forget that not even the government of, by, and for the people can always be trusted to tell the truth. Though most government statements are straightforward enough, the public should beware of tricky wording. And even officials who have hesitated to spread falsehood have on occasion accomplished the same result simply by sweeping the truth under a label of secrecy. Half a story, or no story at all, can be a subtle form of misrepresentation.

Every government tries to control the flow of information to the public and thereby manipulate public opinion. Dictatorships accomplish this simply by seizing newspapers, censoring the news, turning the radio-TV industry into a propaganda network, and jailing recalcitrant writers.

In democracies, the leaders must be more subtle, their news management more sophisticated. Yet they are every bit as eager to softsoap the public for the noble purpose, in their view, of perpetuating themselves in power.

In this country, Presidents usually have sought to influence the news by influencing the men who write and publish it. President Johnson hugged newsmen to his bosom and overwhelmed them with the facts he wanted them to print. These depicted national issues, not necessarily as they were, but as he wanted the nation to see them. Newsmen who couldn't be pampered would be pressured. LBJ would bring all the pressures of the presidency to bear on them. He would go over their heads to their publishers who might be more susceptible to presidential flattery. He would also intimidate the sources of news. His tantrums over unauthorized news leaks terrorized those who had once talked freely Upon occasion, LBJ would even order investigations of correspondents whose writings displeased him.

President Nixon has been more open and honest in dealing with the press. However, he has unleashed Vice President Agnew who attacked the networks for criticizing the President's Vietnam speech. The bombast had the desired result: there was no criticism whatever of Nixon's next network appearance. Agnew immediately followed up with a broadside against *The Washington Post* and *The New York Times*, which aren't so easily intimidated. Intimates say that Agnew privately balked at attacking the great networks and newspapers. He suspected that the President was setting him up as a target to draw their fire away from himself.

But Richard Nixon, as calculating a politican as has ever reached the White House, has a far more profound strategy. He seeks to tap the deep undercurrents of uneasiness that are stirring the silent majority, say insiders. Deep in the subterranean soul of Middle America, he has detected a brooding outrage against crime and violence, immorality and anti-Americanism, black power and student dissension. He would like to transform this hidden force into political power.

He also senses that these troubled Americans, deep down, distrust the press which brings them bad news. They are angered over the radicals and militants who always seem to have easy access to the TV cameras.

The reaction to Agnew's speeches, as the President anticipated, was overwhelmingly favorable. The polls showed that an astonishing percentage of the people agreed with Agnew about the networks and newspapers. This made a quick impression upon the network executives, who are always sensitive to public whims as measured by the pollsters. Criticism of the Nixon Administration suddenly became muted on television. And Agnew was able to boast, "Sometimes when I look around at the tube from time to time, I think I have had a modicum of success."

More ominous than the attacks upon the press are the subpoenas the Nixon Administration began issuing for reporters' notes. This strikes at the heart of press freedom, for the sources of information will quickly dry up if the government has the power to pry into newsmen's private files, read their confidential notes and thereby learn the identity of their informants. Without informants to tell about the blunders, waste and corruption that government officials try to cover up, correspondents will be limited largely to the information that the government wishes to divulge. This will make it difficult to contradict, criticize and expose government officials who try to make bad policies look good.

The First Amendment, which guarantees freedom of the press, gives newsmen freedom not only to write what they please but to gather information. The issue is not special privilege for the press but the right of the people to know. The Supreme Court has declared that the First Amendment guarantees "are not for the benefit of the press so much as for the benefit of all of us."

The pressures for conformity, the preference for entertainment over information, the intolerance for certain points of view — these have combined to suppress controversy. Radio and TV producers shy away from controversy as if it were unpatriotic. They hire motivational researchers, statisticians, sociologists, psychologists, and pollsters to make sure they never offend the mass mind. This blandness is dictated, in part, by advertising agencies, which don't like to ruffle the unseen audience. Radio-TV stations, more than newspapers, bow toward Madison Avenue, the advertising Mecca. Even the great networks take care not to offend sponsors who might withdraw a multimillion-dollar account over a political comment not to their liking.

The few telecasters who once may have risked a little controversy were set back by the outcry over Howard K. Smith's documentary, "The Political Obituary of Richard Nixon," after his unsuccessful campaign for the presidency in 1960. The ABC network was struck by a storm of protest, not because the political obituary may have been premature, but because Smith had the impudence to interview Alger Hiss as one of the figures who had played a role in Nixon's life. James Hagerty, ABC's vice president in charge of news, went before the cameras to warn solemnly, "If we are weakened, you are weakened, for if through fear or intimidation, we fail to provide all the news — favorable or unfavorable — then you, the citizens of the nation, cannot be properly informed." But when a couple of right-wing sponsors threatened to take their money and go elsewhere, ABC suddenly forgot all about its duty to inform. The front office kicked Hagerty upstairs, ended Smith's experiment in bold journalism, and began censoring the news more closely.

Thanks to such shyness, we are fast becoming a nation of conformists. The vast public, if not brainwashed, has had its gray tissue thoroughly rinsed. It has succumbed to the techniques of the advertising agencies, whose pitchmen in pinstripes seem able to promote laxatives, deodorants, and presidential candidates with equal know-how.

There is a subtle menace in too much conformity, in the government's "Uncle knows best" attitude. The democratic machinery should never run so smoothly and silently that the rumble of opposition becomes muffled. Let there be a few cogs that grate against the massive wheels of Big Government, Big Business, and Big Labor.

THE PRESS — A SLEEPING WATCHDOG

Traditionally the press has been charged with the job of monitoring the ethical conduct of public officials in this country, a job it has failed to do with spectacular consistency. Its lack of diligence in this regard is perhaps best illustrated by newspaper coverage of personal expense funds raised to help two prominent Senators in recent years — Thomas Dodd and Richard Nixon. More money was contributed to Dodd's personal fund between 1958 and 1967 than to Nixon's while he was running for Vice President in 1952, but the principle involved was similar. The punishment, however, was not. Dodd was censured by the Senate despite an emotional appeal to his peers. Nixon made a similar emotional appeal to the American people on television, and was elected Vice President of the United States. Probably the basic reason for the differing outcomes to the cases was the way the press reported the stories.

An account of Nixon's $18,000 personal expense fund, contributed by 76 of his friends, was first published September 18, 1952, by the *New York*

Post and the *Los Angeles Daily News,* both with Democratic editorial policies (the latter is now defunct). A revelation of this kind would normally have rocked the nation. No such slush fund had ever figured in a Presidential race. Yet Midwest newspapers, almost all of them Republican in their editorial affiliation, smothered the story so completely that the general public scarcely understood the seriousness of the charge against the Republican candidate for Vice President.

The *Omaha World-Herald,* for instance, printed the story on page 56 and used a headline that made it appear that Nixon was the beneficiary of an insurance trust fund.

With the exception of the *St. Louis Post-Dispatch,* a Democratic paper, no newspaper subsequently dug into the ramifications of the Nixon fund and demonstrated the benefits that had been received by those who secretly contributed to it.

Under the rules of Congress, a member is at liberty to help his constituents, but at no time is he entitled to receive remuneration for any representation he makes before the United States Government. A member of the Congress is a servant of the Government, paid by it and not by private individuals. He is required, furthermore, to serve all his constituents without favor, not merely those who secretly contribute funds to help defer his expenses. But the Nixon case was marked by gratitude expressed in the form of campaign contributions for favors done and votes cast while he had served in Congress.

Lethargy on the part of the press undoubtedly contributed to another bizarre money-raising scheme in 1960 when the Nixon family was again involved in a flagrant conflict of interest. On October 25, as the Kennedy-Nixon campaign was moving down the homestretch, it was revealed in a syndicated news column ("Washington Merry-Go-Round" written at the time by Drew Pearson and Jack Anderson) that Nixon's brother Don had received a $205,000 loan on December 10, 1956, from Howard Hughes, the airplane manufacturer who was then chief stockholder of Trans World Airlines. The loan, secured by a mortgage on Lot 10 on Whittier Boulevard in Whittier, California — a piece of real estate that no bank would have accepted as security for a loan of that size — was apparently never repaid. The Hughes Tool Company was an important defense contractor. TWA had applied for an extension of its route from the Philippines to Japan. Hughes himself faced an antitrust suit, and he had other problems, none of which were likely to become aggravated by the fact that the family of Richard Nixon, a man who might become President of the United States, was beholden to him financially.

Again, a large number of newspapers failed to exercise their role as watchdog for the public. Subsequently, New England newspapers selected three veteran newsmen — Norman Isaacs, editor of the *Louisville Courier-Journal;* Carl Lindstrom, editor of the *Hartford Times* and author of the book *The Fading American Newspaper*; and Edward Rowse of *The Washington Post* — to survey why they were losing influence with the public. The panel picked the Nixon-Hughes loan story as a case in point and reported that of the 43 New England papers that had normally run the Pearson-Anderson column, only three had run the column that broke the Hughes loan story.

"There was no wire-service treatment of the loan story until late in the day of October 26," the editorial panel reported. The Associated Press lead was a strong denial of the column by Robert Finch, Nixon's Washington campaign manager, who called the story "an obvious political smear" and denied the loan was from Hughes. The United Press International also carried Finch's denial, but farther down in the story. Despite the availability of these two wire-service accounts, the three editors noted, 19 of the 43 papers being examined passed up the news story.

When the wire services carried a story on October 28 saying that the Justice Department denied that the loan to Donald Nixon was in any way linked to its having dropped an antitrust suit against the Hughes Tool Company, the *Providence Journal* headlined it "JUSTICE DEPARTMENT NAILS PEARSON CHARGE." The *Boston-American* headline read "WRITER HIT IN NIXON SMEAR TRY."

In a follow-up that was sent out for distribution October 27, "Washington Merry-Go-Round" charged that the Nixons had gone to great lengths to keep the Hughes loan a secret and to avoid paying capital gains taxes on the difference between the purchase price of the property in 1923, $4,000, and the $205,000 sale price taxable at 25 per cent — or $50,250. The *Portsmouth Herald* was the only New England newspaper to run the follow-up column.

In the panel's judgment, the matter of news censorship "passed beyond any debate stage on October 30 when the AP sent a dispatch from Los Angeles at 5:38 P.M. reporting that Donald Nixon had admitted that the $205,000 loan had originated from the Hughes Tool Company. But nothing of this could be located in nine of the (New England) morning papers." A later, fuller AP story moved on October 30, reported that Finch admitted he was misinformed when he had at first denied that the loan came from Hughes. "The Finch story raises a problem," the panel of editors went on. "Twenty-two papers did not carry the first wire stories in which Finch denounced Pearson's charges. But what of the 21 newspapers which had carried the earlier Finch denials? Giving thoughtful weight to the principle of equity of news treatment, the committee can find no excuse to justify the omission of the October 30 Finch (admission) statement by these 21 newspapers."

Thus, here was a man running for President of the United States whose brother had received a loan of almost a quarter of a million dollars from a top government contractor under circumstances no responsible bank would countenance, yet the majority of the Republican-owned newspapers in one thoroughly analyzed sector of the nation either suppressed the news or carried denials of the truth. Though Nixon went on to the Presidency in 1968, newspapers again have not bothered to report that the Nixon family lot is now registered in the name of the Hughes Tool Company.

The story of Senator Dodd's personal expense fund in all its ramifications was aired rather fully by the press, but only after the Senate Ethics Committee swung into action. The wide press coverage presumably contributed to public pressure on the Senate to censure Dodd. The one place in the country where news of the case was suppressed was the Senator's home state of Connecticut, where the press is inclined to be Democratic or to favor a local boy. Robert H. Yoakum, a Connecticut resident and frequent contributor to the *Columbia Journalism Review*, surveyed the press coverage of the Dodd case in Connecticut and concluded, "If ever a man had reason to be grateful to the press, that man is Thomas J. Dodd."

Yoakum, noting the indifference of the 1,400-man Washington press and broadcasting corps, reported that "in the three months from the first Pearson-Anderson column on January 24, 1966, until the Ethics Committee announced hearings on April 29, 1966, the Dodd employees (who offered evidence against Dodd) were interviewed by only two people: Sarah McClendon, representing some Texas newspapers, and James Canan of the Gannett Newspapers, which take in the *Hartford Times*." The wire services were hardly more conscientious than the newspapers, Yoakum added, remarking that the UPI's dispatches "often sounded as though they had been processed in Dodd's office: 'For eight years, he has been one of the most respected members of the Senate,' a UPI background story reported inaccurately in April 1966, compounding the error later in the piece by referring to Dodd as '. . .a man respected for his views on foreign affairs.'" His indignation rising, Yoakum wrote, "A Senator was up to his clavicle in ill-gained dollars, but the wire services were unable to spring even one of their 141 Washington reporters to interview the ex-employees who had the story."

Lax as the press has been over the years, vulnerable as it has been to charges of lethargy and even self-servicing distortion of the news — with all this, it has seen the moments of its greatness flare. None in recent years was so brilliant as its decision to make public the "Pentagon Papers," a venture which involved, as an editorial writer for *The Washington Post* (Meg Greenfield) wrote, ". . .a rare and unconventional step on the part of the newspapers involved — an assumption of responsibility at some risk to themselves, a decision to shatter the protocol of government-press arrangements, a refusal to abide by hypocritical standards that do not protect the nation or the public or the fighting men in Vietnam — but which only protect the reputations of some and the complacency of all in regard to the Vietnamese war. Those of us — which includes practically everyone I know moving around these areas of journalism — who have not the smallest inclination to overturn and expose government's legitimately kept secrets, believed this information (the "Pentagon Papers") to be ultimately and only a source of public good if it were to be made known. The constitution contest that ensued was and is of the greatest importance. But so may be the result of publication of the Pentagon documents. It may remind government of its proper function as surrogate for the public; and it has already recalled to the press its essentially private — which is to say, unofficial — role, not as an arm or mouthpiece of government, but rather as an independent instrument of criticism, functioning outside its reach."

FOREIGN POLICY

Uncle Sam's word, once as good as his gold, no longer is trusted around the world. Too many times U.S. spokesmen have resorted to deception which, inevitably, has produced more embarrassment than would have resulted from the incidents they tried to hide. They have been caught in one awkward lie after another until world confidence in Uncle Sam has been severely shaken.

The most recent, and surely the most damaging, instance of this sort of governmental chicanery is the exposure of the infamous "Pentagon Papers," a secret study that was published first by *The New York Times* in June, 1971. The Pentagon's study tells an astounding story of systematic deception practiced at the highest levels of policy making in American government. What perhaps was even more astounding, was the response by the Administration — an attempt by the federal government, for the first time in U.S. history, legally to stop a newspaper from publishing a story.

Before the gag was placed on the *Times* (and later on *The Washington Post*), it became clear that the U.S. had secretly waged war in Laos and North Vietnam from the beginning of 1964; that the Tonkin Gulf incident was used as a pretext to whip Congress into a patriotic froth that brought forth a resolution that the Pentagon had drawn up months before; that President Johnson's war-policy councils were planning the very military moves that Johnson, during his election campaign, was condemning his opponent, Barry Goldwater, for even suggesting; that President Johnson secretly sent ground troops into combat in South Vietnam.

Some people contend that the President, for the protection of the nation, sometimes must withhold the whole truth about foreign affairs. But domestic officials have also played loose with the truth to cover up blunders, hide corruption and make bad policies look good.

The public can be excused for wondering occasionally whom and what to believe. Former Defense Secretary Robert McNamara's continuously optimistic reports on the war in Vietnam, for example, were regularly contradicted by events on the battlefront. The Defense Department's credibility had sunk so low by 1970 that one newsman wrote that "most Pentagon reporters really don't believe a story until it has been officially denied."

Former Pentagon spokesman Arthur Sylvester once contended that "information is a weapon, a very important weapon, to be used or withheld." Though he denied any intent by the government to "phony up" the news, he defended the government's inherent right to "lie to save itself when it's going up into a nuclear war." That this was indeed the position taken by the Johnson Administration is evident in nearly every page of the "Pentagon Papers". It is axiomatic to say that a democracy cannot exist with men who feel they must betray the public for reasons that the public is supposedly too stupid to understand. The position raises the question whether a democracy, in the war of words, should trade in lies. It would appear that the "Pentagon Papers" answer the question. In a democracy, the truth has a habit of bubbling to the surface. Democracy's strength lies in the free flow of accurate information to its citizens. Of course, security information must be withheld from the public, so it won't reach an enemy, but in these cases, a simple "no comment" is better than a lie.

Yet, increasingly, American policymakers have engaged in the disturbing practice of concocting "cover stories," as official lies are delicately called. Unhappily, the covers have repeatedly been ripped off these stories and the exposure has always been, at the very least embarrassing. The "Pentagon Papers" were only the latest embarrassment; there have been many others.

Six days after a U-2 spy plane disappeared over Russia in 1960, the State Department blandly announced, "There was no deliberate attempt to violate Soviet airspace, and there has never been." The world soon learned that U-2's had been winging over Russia for several years. The following year, the late Adlai Stevenson, relying on information from Washington, lied to the United Nations about the Bay of Pigs invasion. Another who helped spread misinformation about this debacle was White House aide Arthur Schlesinger, Jr., who, in his memoirs, presented a different set of facts from those he gave to *The New York Times* in 1961. When his book disclosed the size of the invasion force was 1,400 men, the *Times* reminded him of his claim to them that no more than 200 to 300 men were involved.

"Did I say that?" blurted Schlesinger. "Well, I was lying. This was a cover story."

During the Cuban missile crisis a year later, government information was tightly controlled and carefully coordinated to give a false picture. Five days after aerial photographs were taken of Soviet missiles in Cuba, for example, the Pentagon issued the following statement to newsmen: "A Pentagon spokesman denied tonight that any alert has been ordered or that any emergency measures have been set in motion against communist-ruled Cuba." Though not a word of this was true, Pentagon press chief Arthur Sylvester still insisted three months later, "There has been no distortion, no deception, and no manipulation of the news released by the Defense Department during the Cuban crisis."

In the 1965 Dominican Republic uprising, a whole series of conflicting stories were put out. At first Washington announced that U.S. forces had been sent to protect the lives of American citizens. Later, it was admitted that the purpose was to prevent a communist takeover. The government released a list of 58 Reds said to be active on the rebel side. Reporters quickly found that the list not only included duplications, but contained the names of men then in prison or out of the country.

"If a government repeatedly resorts to lies in crises where lies seem to serve its interests best, it will one day be unable to employ the truth effectively when the truth would serve its interests best," warns J. Russell Wiggins, editor of *The Washington Post*. "A government that too readily rationalizes its right to lie in a crisis will never lack for either lies or crises."

THE STATE DEPARTMENT

The State Department is the key agency in the day-to-day routine of foreign relations. It carries the burden of responsibility, a burden reflected in its somewhat stodgy personality. The late President Kennedy, exasperated over the State Department's constant caution, its nagging fear of making a mistake, called it "a bowl of jelly." He grumped, "They never have any ideas over there, never come up with anything new." President Johnson, even less successful at budging the diplomats, once said despairingly he'd like to fire everybody and start over. Former Ambassador John Bartlow Martin remembers the Department as "a vast bulky obscure antagonist," and Senate Foreign Relations Chairman J. William Fulbright sees it as "an immobile, impenetrable bureaucracy." Junior diplomats, mired in its sluggish procedures, speak of it as "the fudge factory."

To many insiders, the State Department seems to be geared to deferring decisions and resisting suggestions. A new idea is at once ensnared in red tape, interred under paper and entombed in a padlocked steel filing cabinet. It's also a rare foreign service officer who will put his views in writing without carefully hedging. He has learned to keep a wary eye upon the second guessers in Congress and to phrase his reports so they reflect safe, if not always honest, opinions. As the Department maxim puts it, "There are old foreign service officers and bold foreign service officers, but there are no old, bold foreign service officers."

This doesn't deter them from writing reports. Indeed, the less they have to say, the more words they require to say it. Every day, the State Department is struck by a blizzard of paper — more than 10,000 messages which must be copied, distributed and filed. To read, let alone digest, them all is an undertaking that threatens to bog down the diplomatic machinery. "The chief beneficiary," suggested H. Freeman Matthew, a former career ambassador, "may well be the eye doctor."

The Foreign Service also seems to operate largely for the benefit of the Foreign Service. Our diplomats are rotated more to suit their own convenience than the national need. The pleasant posts, such as Paris, London, Bonn, and Vienna, are overstaffed and overstuffed. The disagreeable places all too often are neglected. The diplomatic set also tends to congregate in golden ghettos, to talk to the same people at the same cocktail parties, to reflect the innate attitudes of their set.

All this has blunted the effectiveness of the State Department, whose vital mission it is to keep the planet Earth from being blown up. Its diplomacy will determine how much the citizens are taxed, whether their children will be drafted and perhaps killed. It promotes peace on a cut-rate $456 million annual budget. There is no service more important to the American people who, unfortunately, are inclined to take peace, like health, for granted until it is suddenly lost. Yet our harried diplomats, who may have no trouble explaining U.S. policy to a Zanzibar chieftain in his native Swahili, are curiously unable to communicate with Congress and the public. They do a poor job of diplomacy on Capitol Hill — though admittedly they have no constituency, no industrial complex, no high-pressure lobby to help fight their Congressional battles. Result: the diplomatic service is generally scorned by politicians, scoffed at by the press, suspected by the public.

This has caused a decrease in State Department support, a decay in morale and a decline in American foreign policy. Into the vacuum has rushed the Pentagon's brass hats and the CIA's operators, who have been conducting their own brand of foreign policy in many countries. The situation became so chaotic that President Kennedy in 1961 issued a directive giving the ambassadors full authority over military attaches and CIA agents. This reduced, though never halted, their depredations into State's territory. One strategem employed by the CIA is to direct an operation in Burma, say, from next-door Thailand. The CIA doesn't bother to clear it with the ambassador to Thailand, since he has nothing to say about what goes on in Burma. The Ambassador to Burma, on the other hand, has no authority over the CIA in Thailand.

State is the nation's senior department, founded by the First Congress ahead of any domestic Cabinet office. The Secretary "was not so much overcharged with business," it was decided, that his five clerks couldn't handle a few domestic chores, too. Today, State has 24,285 employees which, despite its seniority, makes it the second smallest department (only Labor is smaller).

The heart of the State Department is its diplomatic service. This is operated by the professional career men — 3,110 of them scattered among 25 embassies, consulates general and consulates around the world. Harassed and hamstrung though they may be, most of them put in long hours and give dedicated service. Some also endure hardships unknown in America since pioneer times. They may live in mud huts on the Equator, work in drafty quarters above the Arctic Circle, travel to the dead ends of the earth. They may face death from rioting mobs and exotic diseases. Their wives may be obliged to sit cross-legged with them on the floor, eating chicken entrails with a native leader, while their children attend a primitive school. For all this, they are paid a lower starting salary than is the bus driver who delivers them to the State Department building.

The diplomats in the field deal chiefly with the desk officers who watch and analyze events in each country. From all over the world, coded reports flood into the State Department by telegram, diplomatic pouch and scrambled phone circuit. Most of the messages are dumped into the in-boxes of the appropriate desk officers. The top policymakers have time to read only the most urgent telegrams. Aware of this and anxious to attract notice, the ambassadors generally upgrade their trivia and send it by urgent telegram. To break through to the White House, former Ambassador J. K. Galbraith has suggested, it helps to include a four-letter word in the telegram.

The telegrams hum into the Operations Center over teletypes housed in soundproof cabinets. Mysterious machines with winking lights code and decode the secret messages. The most timely telegrams are attached to clipboards beneath wall maps of the troubled areas. Overhead is a row of wall clocks, giving the exact time in the chief world capitals. Other messages are hurried by hand or shot by pneumatic tubes to the bureaus and country desks. For the top brass, a telecon can flash incoming messages upon a screen in the conference room.

This irresistible paper flow engulfs the frenzied bureaucrats who struggle manfully to channel it. Because of its sheer volume, they don't pretend to read everything. Indeed, most of the reports, if noted at all, are filed away unheeded. One foreign service officer, if he had no solution for the problem, at least was able to reduce it to a theorem: "Every producer of paper added to the payroll creates the need for an additional consumer of paper."

But the consumers also become producers, thus creating the need for still more consumers. This bureaucratic chain reaction is more common, of course, at the glamorous European embassies. The Foreign Service is dominated by diplomats of the European school who are inclined to pay more attention to a reception in Paris than a revolution in Paraguay. The State Department keeps 58 people in Austria, only 5 in Angola. Yet the potential for trouble would seem to be greater in racially tense Angola. At the Paris embassy, 4 people are assigned to the agriculture attache's office alone to report on French farming. In Nairobi, a single attache and a secretary once tried to keep up with the agriculture of seven countries. Now even they have been withdrawn.

Ellis O. Briggs, a career ambassador, is convinced that most embassies could perform twice as effectively with half the personnel. When he headed the Athens embassy, he had 70 military aides, attaches and other specimens underfoot. "Had I been able to deploy them for three hours every morning in full-dress uniform, playing leapfrog across the Acropolis," he said, "that would have made as much sense as most of the attache duties they solemnly declared they were engaged in."

The more people who work on a project, each trying to justify his salary, the longer it takes to complete. Another erstwhile ambassador, William Attwood, writing in the *Atlantic*, declared, "Ten people will spend 20 man-hours preparing a paper that one able man could prepare in two."

The State Department has devised an insidious system of clearances and concurrences which keeps more and more people busy accomplishing less and less. Action papers must be initialed by so many officials that they look like petitions. Ambassador Matthew complained that too many people "feel they have a vested interest in most subjects that come up. But the more people and the more proliferation of committees there are, the more difficult it is to come up with a decision."

The no-sayers and nitpickers quickly pluck all the feathers out of a new idea. Their reasoning is that a new approach not only would mean revision of all the old paperwork, but could raise awkward questions about the old ideas they had defended. They find it simpler to route the new proposal around in concentric circles.

No matter is too trivial to get the route-around. One eager, young foreign service officer, assigned to type file cards, quickly figured a way to speed up the work. He submitted his suggestion, but nothing happened. "So I started asking around," he said. "First thing I found out was how many people had experienced the same kind of thing."

One who tried to buck the system said hopelessly, "You try to hit it, change it, yell at it, but it seems to go on undisturbed and largely untouched." Ambassador Briggs described how he had struggled for six months to reduce his embassy staff in Czechoslovakia. "It exhausts me to remember the struggle with Washington required to obtain a reduction from 80 to 78 persons," he recalled. "If I had started to dig the projected Nicaraguan Canal with a teaspoon, those six months might have shown a more impressive achievement." Czechoslovakia's communist government unwittingly came to his aid by ordering most of his staff out of the country. "They possibly thought they were dealing the American Ambassador the most painful blow imaginable," he said, "when they suddenly declared five-sixths of my staff *persona non grata.*" Happily, he sent them packing and got along with a staff of 12. His first secretary doubled as an economist and propagandist. Another foreign service officer drove the embassy truck when he wasn't at his desk. Boasted Briggs, "The State Department, after it recovered from the shock, declared it was delighted with the Embassy's performance."

Not even the Secretary of State can always impose his decisions upon the Foreign Service he is supposed to command. Ambassador Martin once tried to get more visa officers to clear up "a visa mess" in the Dominican Republic. He took up his problem with State's top brass. "Incredibly," he reported, "I had to ask the Secretary (Dean Rusk) himself to resolve it. He was wholly sympathetic, and said we should send a planeload of young visa officers to the Republic immediately. But as so often happens, that juggernaut, the State Department, overruled the Secretary just as the Department by sheer inertia sometimes overruled the President."

The career official remains largely oblivious to the demands from on top, secure in the knowledge that he will be sitting at the same desk, initialing the same papers, after the secretariat has been replaced. "Even the President," said Martin, is at the mercy of the old hands — the "old Dominican hands, old China hands, old Cuba hands." The policymaker "will disregard them at his peril. But he may heed them to his sorrow," said Martin. "For all too often their expertise derives from long ago and sometimes irrelevant experience."

Those skilled at bureaucratic intrigue are more likely to get ahead than those trained at foreign intrigue. Career development and personal convenience are put ahead of foreign relations. Not wishing to be stuck in some forsaken outpost, foreign service officers have devised a rotation system that keeps them from getting thoroughly acquainted with any country. Just as they reach the point of understanding a country and sending home useful reports, they are packed off to a new assignment. The blur of U.S. envoys who pass through a country also leaves about as lasting an impression as a passing express train.

During Ambassador Briggs' 37 years in the Foreign Service, he occupied 17 different posts. Our diplomats have been criticized for not always being able to negotiate with foreign leaders in their own language, but it would take a remarkable linguist to learn the languages of 17 countries.

Briggs recalled that his Soviet counterpart in one European capital was an ill-mannered, unlaundered fellow, who had a disturbing habit of pinching elegant ladies. But a fellow ambassador explained to Briggs, "Yuri may not be smart, but he has been here so long that automatically he does not make mistakes. Under the table, he may pinch the wife of the Minister of Posts and Telegraphs, but you will notice he does not pinch the wife of the Minister of National Defense." Briggs concluded that, in diplomacy, there is no substitute for experience.

Most American diplomats have mastered the social graces, but some display a snobbishness that can be just as offensive as Yuri's crudeness. They have a tendency to look upon lesser mortals as if through invisible monocles. Some also seem to have the impression that champagne and caviar enhance their sophistication. "You can go to three or four cocktail parties every night of the week and see the same people," said one foreign service officer.

The public impression of a diplomat, dressed in striped pants, a cultivated finger curled around the stem of a cocktail glass, generally is not true. But the finest liquors, tax-free and free-flowing, are not always easy to resist. More than one American diplomat, not wishing to seem unappreciative of his host's national beverages, has had to be carried home from a diplomatic doing. One was hustled back to Washington after he tried to address a banquet in Geneva with a tongue so thick he was incoherent. He told reporters that he had been suffering from an abscessed tooth, but his record indicated that the tooth must have been bothering him for years.

The attacks on the Foreign Service have been so frequent, and often unfair, that it has driven our embattled diplomats into a turtle shell. They never know whether the next barb will come from Congress or the Kremlin. The late Senator Joe McCarthy (R-Wis.), unable to cope with the complexities of our age, unable to understand the discrepancy between America's tremendous military might and its diplomatic inability to control events, made the State Department a national scapegoat. Many Americans still regard it as a sanctuary for traitors, homosexuals and fuzzy thinkers.

In 1951, for example, Ambassador Foy Kohler submitted this appraisal of Russia's ability to dominate Red China: "If we take a really long view, I believe we must conclude that it is unthinkable that the Chinese people, over any extended period of time, would be satisfied to remain slaves and victims of a foreign regime." To rigid anticommunists, this view was heretical, and Kohler was pilloried for saying it. He survived to become Ambassador to Russia and to see his prediction come true. But other dedicated diplomats, who had also believed it their duty to give their honest views, were hounded out of government by McCarthy's shotgun charges. "I have seen men's careers set aback and, in fact, busted," Roving Ambassador Averell Harriman has said, "because they held the right views at the wrong time, or for accurately reporting facts that were not popular at the time."

The Foreign Service has never fully recovered from McCarthyism. "Until I came here," said one junior diplomat, "I never placed my ideas in such cautious language."

"Last week," declared another, "I wrote one of my most important documents and I didn't put down everything I believed."

"I have learned not to be open, not to be candid," said another.

"As the old proverb says," added yet another, "it is better to say nothing a thousand times than to say something once and be wrong."

The resulting obfuscation generated by the State Department justifies some of the jokes about its location in Foggy Botton.

There are those, like the able Washington pundit Stewart Alsop, who plead that the way to improve our foreign relations is to "let the poor old Foreign Service alone." The State Department needs a sound, severe, therapeutic, top-to-bottom shake-up. Then let it get about the business of conducting foreign affairs in a forthright manner.

THAT'S THE WAY THE
MONEY GOES. . .

By the end of the 1960's big government was spending more than $200 billion a year to operate; that's roughly 25 cents out of every dollar earned in the United States. The money comes from the taxpayer under various guises as individual income tax, corporation income tax, excise taxes, and customs duties.

To be precise, the U.S. budget dollar for fiscal year 1970 broke down this way: 45 cents came from the individual income tax, 24 cents from the social insurance tax and various contributions, 19 cents from corporation income tax, 8 cents from excise taxes, and 4 cents from other sources too vague to mention.

Where did that dollar go? 22 cents went to the social insurance trust funds; 41 cents to national defense (13 of which was consumed by the Vietnam war); 12 cents to education and other social programs; 4 cents to veterans; 2 cents to international uses; 6 cents for interest on debt; 2 cents to debt reduction; and 11 cents as an operating margin.

That, at any rate, is where it went on paper. Within each of those categories is an area of wasted tax monies that would appall our thrifty ancestors; wastes that, if eliminated along with loopholes, could reduce the present income tax rate by 50 per cent.

The federal government consumes cash at the rate of $220,000 a minute. Every disappearing dollar is painfully extracted from the long-suffering taxpayer who, if the truth were known, doesn't really begrudge money for the nation's needs, but is dismayed to see it wasted. Nevertheless, appalling sums are regularly squandered. Misspent millions have gone down the Pentagon drain like so much green cabbage. More millions have disappeared into the pockets of foreign potentates from Afghanistan to Zanzibar. Countless dollars have been burned, buried, blown to the winds, and blasted into space with there's-more-where-that-came-from abandon.

Millionaires have been subsidized and the poor have been bureaucratically ignored. In the scramble for a place at the federal trough, the rich have juggled their books while others have resorted to less sophisticated duplicity. In 1968 (the latest figures available), 31 persons in the United States paid zero taxes on over $1 million incomes; 538 who made over $100,000 didn't pay anything either.

The greatest offender in terms of spending, of course, is the one with the greatest cut of the budget pie, the Defense Department, the Pentagon. In secret House testimony, Vice Admiral Hyman Rickover has laid bare how greedy defense contractors and bumbling Pentagon officials conspire to cheat the taxpayers. In an 88-page transcript that found its way into the hands of newsmen, the tart-tongued Admiral describes how the taxpayers' money disappears down the Pentagon drain.

He charged that "a small group of self-perpetuating men shuffle back and forth through industry, government, Washington law offices and the lobbies" to keep the taxpayers' gold flowing. He cited these examples:

One large shipbuilder with a $70-million contract tried to collect another $70 million in extras. To support the claim, the company submitted "dozens of file cabinets" loaded with documents. Alleged Rickover, "The government simply did not have enough people to review the claim in detail." It was settled, he said, "at about 90 per cent of the amount the contractor claimed."

Another contractor reported a 9 per cent profit when the true figures would have shown an 802 per cent profit. Still another company squeezed a 573 per cent return on its net investment out of a defense contract.

The Justice Department settled a $300,000 overcharge against a Navy contractor at eight cents on the dollar. The Department accepted this penny ante offer, complained Rickover, without bothering to consult the Navy.

International Nickel Co., a Canadian firm doing 60 per cent of the world's nickel business, "avoids the Truth-in-Negotiations Act" on its defense contracts, he charged, while reaping "record profits." He added that a shipbuilder's team of 75 men who are specialists at scalping the government is paid, incredibly, by the government itself.

He also testified that the giant computer industry thumbs its nose at government reporting regulations, all the while raking in $3 billion a year from the federal government.

"The Department of Defense has come to be essentially a regulatory body whose function it is to protect the industries it is dealing with," grumped the Admiral. His own attempts to cut costs for the taxpayers, he said, invariably met with pussyfooting and pigeonholing. For example, he implored Assistant Secretary of the Navy Frank Sanders to do something about a gigantic shipping firm which was overcharging the government. Rickover's classified report to Sanders detailed fast shuffles "in the design, construction and overhaul of nuclear submarines."

Interrupted Chairman Brooks, "Admiral, have other officials in the Navy seen this report you mentioned? Is something being done about it?"

"My reports were received by my superiors, in general, in the manner one would historically expect," the Admiral replied caustically. "They started an investigation which will be conducted by the very people who for years had been responsible for the situation."

At another point, Brooks said, "I do not understand how a company can survive with these practices."

"They couldn't," agreed Rickover, "except for one thing. It is the government's money they are wasting, not their own."

The peppery old Admiral said the Truth-in-Negotiations Act, which is supposed to keep contractors honest, "brings neither truth nor negotiations."

"How," asked Brooks, "do contractors react to this law?"

"In some cases," said the Admiral, "there seems to be an industry-wide policy not to comply... Their argument seems to be, 'We have been breaking the law for many years, therefore we have established this as a right.'"

He charged that the Defense Department aids and abets the contractors as they "juggle their cost and profit figures."

"An onlooker would have difficulty determining which negotiators are from the government and which are from industry," he said. Then he added from experience, "One should not accept a blind date nor a contractor's report without checking them."

Rickover claimed that the Renegotiation Board, which is supposed to monitor the $60 billion in government contracts, has only 184 employees and is "about as effective as putting a Band-Aid on cancer." Result: "Nobody at the Pentagon can tell you exactly how much profit contractors make."

"What has the Pentagon done about it?" demanded Brooks.

"The Department of Defense," retorted Richover, "is attacking the problem in typical bureaucratic fashion. They are studying the situation. The word 'study' in the Department of Defense is a euphemism for inaction or delay." Then the old Admiral sounded this solemn warning: "People will not tolerate high profits on war contracts while their young sons are being drafted to risk their lives for their country."

WHY BOTHER?

In some small support of Rickover's charges, comes the plight of CEA Industries, a small company in the Washington suburbs, which is finding that while saving the government money may be popular with the taxpayers it can get you in trouble with the bureaucrats. When the company earned more than expected on an Army contract, it tried to give the government back $2,000. Company president Frank Wood, recalling his meeting with Army officials, said ruefully, "They practically laughed me out of the place." Government officials argue that it might well have cost the government more than $2,000 in paperwork just to accept the refund.

Now the company's thrifty ways have produced new bureaucratic bafflement. CEA submitted the low bid to build a tourist exhibit for the Treasury Department. This $21,000 bid was half what the Department had expected the project to cost and $11,000 below the second lowest offer. Astonished Treasury officials, suspicious of such a bargain, immediately offered Wood the chance to withdraw his bid. When he declined, a delegation from the Department showed up at his plant in Fairfax, Va., and demanded to be shown around. Since Wood was absent, they returned the following day, inspected the plant, and discussed the contract at length. Wood and his staff assured the Treasury officials that CEA could easily handle the job. The next day, the contract was awarded to the Philadelphia firm which had bid more than $32,000. William Boteler, the Treasury official responsible for the decision, explained to newsmen that the Philadelphia company got the contract because his department feared CEA couldn't do the work. "His bid was so low that he could not have had an understanding of the project," said Boteler.

Comptroller General Elmer Staats, the government's watchdog on spending, is supposed to uncover fiscal irregularities — not cover them up. In February, 1971, his auditors, after checking 146 military contracts, had found that the contractors had been giving false figures. The contractors' reports to the Pentagon had claimed profits on equity investment of 21.1 per cent; Staats' sleuths had found their actual profits were 56.1 per cent.

Instead of announcing this shocking news to the public, Staats slipped around to the Pentagon and tipped off the defense contractors what his auditors had discovered. One auditor, fearing Staats would next alter the findings, slipped a copy of the confidential draft survey to the press. His fears were justified. The military lobby succeeded in gutting the report that finally was released to the public.

The defense contractors were downright distressed over the disclosure that they had been pocketing more than double the profits they had been reporting to the Pentagon. They were also mightily upset over the auditors' demand for an overhaul of the whole contract accounting system. Staats obligingly has rewritten the condemning report. On February 26, a new draft was printed up. Like the first, is was "Restricted to Official Use" with a dire warning against divulging the contents to unauthorized people.

But Staats, once again, slipped confidential copies to the defense contractors. When reporters learned of this they called Staats' office and asked for a copy, suggesting that the taxpayers who foot the defense bills have more of a right to the information than the contractors who are under investigation. A spokesman, Roland Sawyer, conceded that the military-industrial trade organizations had been given copies, but he refused to furnish the press with one. From other sources, however, copies were obtained.

Staats' hatchet work had been effective. Some figures were killed entirely, a demand for reform was hidden deep in the text, and the emphasis was shifted to make the contractors' phony figures look valid. Indeed, the new version was based on the same figures that the original report thoroughly discredited. The focus was on the contractors' false figures, not on the true figures dug out by Staats' own auditors. The old honest figures, once the highlight of Chapter 2, were still found in the new version, but they were buried in Chapter 5 and completely ignored in the "Findings and Conclusions."

In the original version, the auditors had demanded guidelines that "stress return on capital in determining profits" — a system that might show up hidden military profits. In Staats' rewrite, this sentence has been cut out of the formal recommendations. An entire section, showing how contractors faked their profit reports, was totally deleted from the report. The new version also gave the impression that the 146-contract audit went beyond the intent of Congress, but the original legislation states clearly that the Comptroller General can "audit and inspect" any contractor's books and can even "issue subpoenaes" to force reluctant industrialists to comply.

The auditors' suppressed findings confirmed Admiral Hyman Rickover's testimony that "cost and profit information furnished by contractors cannot be relied upon unless it has been verified by government auditors." The scrappy little Admiral told Congressmen that in one typical contract he found a 22.77 per cent profit, although the company claimed it would make only 7.5 per cent.

New weapons are supported by a formidable lobby, composed of the brass hats who want them, the contractors who manufacture the component parts, the workers who put them together and the Congressmen whose districts enjoy the economic benefits. It was this combined pressure on poor Staats that compelled him to alter the findings of his auditors.

WHEELER-DEALERS

A staggering $300 million of the taxpayers' money was dished out in 1969 by the various agencies of the federal government for brand new equipment which the agencies found in 1970 they could not use An investigation revealed that the biggest squanderer was the Pentagon, whose purchases of unneeded material accounted for at least 85 per cent of the total.

Typical among the foul-ups was an Army request for 149 combat helmets for U.S. troops in Thailand that somehow became garbled and resulted instead in the purchase of more than, $1,000 worth of olive green football helmets. Sheepish Army officials said only that an effort was made to find another federal agency with a need for football helmets.

Elsewhere in the military, the Navy had 18 unused in-flight aircraft refueling kits which cost the public $45,000. These are sitting in a supply center in Norfolk, Va., waiting to be claimed by some other federal department. The Navy also had 44 guided missile fins it didn't need. They are worth $14,784 and, presumably, are available to any other federal department that may have some finless missiles.

The list of unnecessary equipment — much of it new — that has been found in various military installations in just the first month of 1970 was several hundred pages long. The brand-new equipment ranges from 612 pairs of women's slacks worth more than $2,000 to an electric food warmer valued at $2,000, not to mention a dizzying array of costly electronic and radio gear.

Fortunately for the taxpayers, the millions carelessly tossed about by the Pentagon on unneeded equipment doesn't entirely go to waste. The General Services Administration has about 325 workers across the country who specialize in finding use inside and outside the government for the goods the military can't use. According to GSA officials, more than half of the excess equipment is turned over to other federal departments or to state institutions. Afterwards, the leftovers are put up for sale to the general public. Those goods usually go at bargain prices well below what was initially paid for the equipment. Although the GSA is justifiably proud of its efficiency in cleaning up after the Pentagon, no one in the agency argues that it would not be better to avoid the kind of haphazard purchasing practices which produce these vast quantities of excess new material every year.

In addition to disposing of unusable new goods, the GSA also is charged with helping to get rid of excess used equipment and real estate for federal departments. The frantic pace of the arms race has produced some extraordinary GSA missions. For example, when a generation of Atlas and Titan guided missiles became obsolete a few years ago, the GSA ended up with a bunch of holes in the ground in remote areas of the Dakotas, Colorado and Nevada to try to sell. The holes had been missile silos.

The agency also has been charged with selling or giving away freighters of up to 15 tons, human skeletons, elk, sheep, goats, pigs, shipments of cut timber, piles of sand and crops of grain.

There is a steady flow of old weapons and used motor vehicles. All kinds of airplanes come up for sale and even religious equipment such as portable altars, chalices and altar cloths end up in the surplus hopper. By far the most popular items, say GSA officials, are Jeeps which are snapped up immediately regardless of their condition.

BOON'S BANE

David Boon is one of those "forgotten Americans" who believes in thriftiness with public funds. So he suggested to an Army Incentive Awards committee that money could be saved by buying cars without cigarette lighters. Army drivers aren't supposed to smoke while driving anyway, and the passenger in the front seat, if he is obeying military regulations to wear a seat belt, can't reach the lighter. At $3 to $4 savings on each vehicle, considering the thousands of military vehicles, Boon's idea could save a lot of money. But in this billion-dollar age, the Pentagon has become cavalier about a trifling few hundred thousand dollars.

Sorry, wrote back the Army. "Removal of lighter will not hinder anyone who wants to smoke," Boon was informed by Joseph F. Pisano, executive secretary of the Awards Committee of Tobyhanna Army Depot, Pa. This nonanswer puzzled Boon, since his suggestion was intended to save money, not hinder smokers.

Perhaps Boon, then of Wilkes-Barre, now of Crisfield, Md., is lucky he is not being investigated or fired from his job. That is what happened to Air Force efficiency expert Ernest Fitzgerald when he blew the whistle on military waste.

Whatever the sentiment, the fact is that men of this caliber must appear on the fiscal scene in legion and must cut a wide swath through the knee-deep waste and inefficiency of modern government fiscal practices, waste of the sort that occurred at Cape Kennedy, Florida, when the Air Force wound 136 miles of plastic cable around the site, as "nerves" for the missile firing center. Florida's dampness soon seeped through the insulation, causing a bewildering rash of short circuits. The whole tangled mess had to be replaced by technicians who could have saved the taxpayers over $600,000 by consulting any local electrician.

Procurement officers have a traditionally cavalier attitude toward government funds. Enough is never sufficient; with Oliver Twist-like tenacity, they must have more. The Army once stockpiled 100,000 bottles of embalming fluid, enough to preserve a couple of divisions for eternity. At the same time, the Air Force and Veterans Administration were buying embalming supplies from private firms at a high market price.

Waste reaches its most alarming peak in the military field. The squabble for dollars sometimes seems to occupy the brass hats more than the strategy for defense. They spy on one another, pour out propaganda against each other's weapons, court key Congressmen with every blandishment in the books. Men have died in Vietnam merely to permit one branch of the service to score a point over a sister branch. Staggering amounts have been lavished on armaments that should have been scrapped or never built in the first place.

From generals to carrier admirals, the brass hats have clamored for pet weapons which have turned out to be impractical or obsolete. In some instances their greatest value has been to give some military chief an excuse to demand more money, more men, more gold braid. Occasionally the Defense Department has rushed ahead with new weapons before they have been proven. Its storerooms hold billions of spare parts for canceled and antiquated weapons. "This stuff is about as useful to us as so much junk," Secretary of Defense Robert McNamara once muttered.

Moreover, science has put weapons out of service faster than the advocates have been able to adjust their military thinking. Thus the generals and admirals sometimes have become obsolete along with the weapons they have commanded. On the other hand, the armed forces have produced their share of Billy Mitchells — career officers who have looked ahead to the weapons of the future. Understandably, the advocates of dubious weapons usually fight for them in all sincerity, genuinely believing them to be in the best interests of the country. And some officers argue that it is sometimes necessary to gamble in order not to get left behind in the technological race. However, new weapons have been developed faster than they can be assimilated. Missiles have been sprouting, electronic gadgets blossoming in our technological hothouses. Result: widespread duplication and disorganization.

SOME CASES IN POINT

Perhaps the most grotesque monument to poor planning is the Navy's F3H1 experimental plane. The designers kept adding to the frame until it became too big for the engine. The first planes were so cumbersome they couldn't be flown and had to be carried down the Mississippi on barges.

Another costly mistake, the "Big Dish" radio telescope, depended upon a mammoth precision bearing which scientists found impossible to design. Still they plugged blithely on, submitting optimistic reports the while. Then a trade magazine smelled trouble and reported that the problem of the bearing appeared to be insurmountable. "Who's right about the progress of this project?" a McNamara aide asked the responsible admiral. The admiral resignedly answered, "Send my last report back, and we'll do it over." That was the end of the Big Dish. Money down the drain: $70 million.

The Air Force designed the Goose decoy missile, a pilotless aircraft, to fly at the speed of a B52 and appear on enemy radar screens as a manned bomber. But a major general, with a model of the Goose on his desk, was stumped when he was asked, "How will you synchronize the decoy launchings with the bomber take-offs? And in case of a false alarm, you can call back the bombers; can you bring back the decoys? If not, wouldn't a flight of decoys alert the Russian defenses and bring retaliation?" The general flushed. Nobody had thought of that. Goose was dropped — along with $80 million of the taxpayer's hard cash.

Of all Defense Secretaries, it is generally conceded, McNamara was the toughest with the purse strings. But even he was unable to stop the three services from feuding over weapons and missions. The Army, for instance, tried desperately to get back into the air. In 1962 General Hamilton Howze, a dashing officer given to jump boots and neck scarves, convened a 100-officer Army board which in 90 days came up with recommendations for a full-fledged Army Air Force. The goal: 11,000 aircraft and 20,500 pilots by 1968; 30,000 aircraft and 56,000 pilots by 1975. The Howze board recommendations, officially secret but discreetly leaked, charged that Air Force giant bombers and supersonic fighters didn't meet the Army's battlefield needs. The board called for front-line planes and helicopters to support ground troops. The Air Force answered angrily that Howze was asking for planes too low and slow to survive in jet-infested skies.

Even the head-butting McNamara couldn't prevent the Army from going ahead with its aircarft procurement. He ordered maneuvers to test Army vs. Air Force tactical planes, but Army generals, impatient to grow wings, began testing their planes and helicopters not in mock war, but in real war in South Vietnam. They virtually ignored the Joint Operations Center, established expressly to coordinate all air strikes.

While General Paul Harkins commanded U.S. forces in Vietnam, he was careful not to send vulnerable Army helicopters into major operations without fighter support. But under pressure from Army advocates, he relaxed his orders once and gave field commanders the option of using their own judgment in special circumstances. Here was a loophole for impatient men. A strike was planned against the communist-held village of Ap Bac. Five armed helicopters were sent as escort for 10 banana-shaped troop carriers. They lumbered into deadly machine gun fire. Joint Operations hadn't even been informed of the strike. The first it heard of it was two hours later when a panic call came for fighters. By that time four of the carriers and one armed chopper had been shot down; the others, bullet-riddled, had been driven off. Haunting question: was it right to risk men's lives in the cause of interservice spite?

What came of all this was that in 1966 McNamara ruled that the Army could continue operating its helicopters, but that most of the fixed-wing planes should be turned over to the Air Force.

Before McNamara's reign, when the Air Force was assigned responsibility for strategic bombing, the Navy had tried to cut in on the role. The admirals dreamed up the idea of a jet-powered flying boat, armed with nuclear bombs, which could take off and land wherever there was water. When the Air Force howled foul, the admirals smoothly presented an 18-page paper for the same aircarft disguised as a mine layer. They spent $450 million on the project — $200 million of it prematurely on the production contract — before it was scrapped in 1959. By that time the development of the Polaris had given the Navy a strategic mission. The admirals were content; the taxpayers poorer.

Today top Pentagon officials are taking a hard look at that most sacred of sea cows, the aircraft carrier. A secret defense study claims that sea-based planes, taking into account the cost of their support, cost four times as much as land-based planes. McNamara was known to have favored carriers because they can transfer air power about the world wherever trouble may flare, but now the Marines have developed a prefabricated airfield that can be flown into an area and set up within three days. Uncle Sam can buy 100 of these prefabs for the price of one carrier.

THE GAO'S IMPOSSIBLE DREAM

The preceding section was a quite cursory sketch of a handful of the most obvious waste habits of federal agencies. One must remember that these were the ones that have been discovered. Big government is so complex that there is no way to come up with an absolute dollar figure for wasted taxes. The one agency that is charged with doing just that, however, is the General Accounting Office, the GAO. Its principal function is to oversee the country's bills — to investigate every aspect of the handling of public funds and to report to Congress any hanky-panky or plain mistakes that have been made by a government agency in their handling of those funds.

To this end *The GAO Review* is published every summer (since the office was established in 1921) stuffed with reports of this nature. The 1971 review, for instance, contains this:

We recently reported to Congress a case where the RFC (Reconstruction Finance Corp.) agreed to lease and rehabilitate a privately owned butylene plant at Corpus Christi, Texas, to be operated by a private contractor. This plant was originally constructed by RFC in 1944 at a cost of approximately $8 million. In 1948 it was declared surplus and turned over to General Services Administration for disposal.

GSA, on January 6, 1950, accepted a bid of $756,000, and on May 1, 1950, formally transferred the property to the purchaser. RFC, in October, 1950, agreed to lease the plant at an annual rental of $200,000 until June 30, 1952, with the privilege of a 2-year renewal; to rehabilitate the facilities; and to construct a new gas-recovery unit. The estimate of cost to put this plant back in operation was $1 million but the cost incurred to June 30, 1951, was $2,400,000.

In other words, the Government owned an $8 million plant, sold it for $756,000, leased it back for $200,000 per year, and rehabilitated it to the extent of $2,500,000 — all in the matter of a few months.

So there is a watchdog on duty; his job is overwhelming, but every once in a while he nips somebody's heels. In fact, the GAO was solely responsible for saving the country a total of $250,101,100 in fiscal 1970. The list, published in the comptroller general's annual report, runs to such items as:

"Reduced prices resulting from award of 3-year rather than 1-year contracts for certain operation and maintenance services — Air Force (nonrecurring). . . $32 million."

Almost makes one forget about the $80 million Goose decoy fiasco. Almost, but not quite.